GETTING HIRED

Frances R. Schmidt

Handbook for College Graduates

iUniverse, Inc.
Bloomington

Getting Hired
Handbook for College Graduates

Copyright © 2012 Frances R. Schmidt

iUniverse books may be ordered through booksellers or by contacting:

iUniverse
1663 Liberty Drive
Bloomington, IN 47403
www.iuniverse.com
1-800-Authors (1-800-288-4677)

ISBN: 978-1-4502-9531-4 (sc)
ISBN: 978-1-4502-9529-1 (e)

Library of Congress Control Number: 2011960844

Printed in the United States of America

· iUniverse rev. date: 12/30/2011

Contents

CHAPTER 5   Résumé/CV Basics

CHAPTER 6   How to Prepare Your Résumé/CV

CHAPTER 7   Résumé/CV Reference Guide

CHAPTER 8   Getting Results from Your Portfolio

CHAPTER 9   Writing a Winning Cover Letter

CHAPTER 10   Interview Realities

INTRODUCTION

Give yourself credit for beginning your job search. It is hard work. The process can be difficult and leave you feeling frustrated. It challenges you on many levels and may make your life confusing for a while, since you'll feel the pressure to graduate college and the pressure to get hired at the same time. I encourage you not to short change yourself or your job search. You have earned the opportunity to get hired in any employment market.

My eighteen years' experience serving as director of the D'Youville College Career Services Center in Buffalo, New York, allowed me to help thousands of graduates of all ages prepare to get hired, before and after graduation.

I have learned how difficult it is for college graduates to balance their job search with academics and additional responsibilities. My broad career development background includes helping individuals from all walks of life reach their career and employment goals.

The purpose for writing this book, *Getting Hired: Handbook for College Graduates*, is to save you time, energy, and stress. My mission is to help graduates successfully market themselves to employers so they can make a smooth transition from college to career.

Based on employer feedback and actual job search success stories, I will *show* rather than tell you how to take charge of your job search and get hired in any job market. How you market yourself to employers can make a major difference in the amount of time it takes to get hired. By focusing on the nuts and bolts of the entire hiring process, you'll avoid making mistakes along the way.

This handbook takes the difficult and stressful task of job hunting and breaks it down into manageable pieces. Each chapter provides a realistic framework for all aspects of the job search process, with a focus on the employer's point of view.

Summary of Contents

Chapter 1, "Handling Job Search Stress," will explain how to deal with the emotions that every job searcher must deal with, and it will help you assess your goals at the outset of your search. Chapter 2, "Networking Counts," discusses the importance of networking and shows you how to do it the right way. Chapter 3, "The Job Search Process," explains exactly what is involved in the process. It will help you determine whether an employer would be likely to hire you, and it provides tools to evaluate your online presence. Chapter 4, "Marketing Your Qualifications," provides an overview of the ways we can market ourselves in the workforce. Chapter 5, "The Résumé/CV Basics" chapter, explains the basics of what is included on your résumé or CV. The "Basic Résumé/CV Worksheet" will help you format your document. Chapter 6, "How to Prepare Your Résumé/CV," further discusses how to select your basic format and how to organize your content. Chapter 7, "The Résumé/CV Reference Guide," provides a detailed reference you can use to format your document. The "Sample Résumé/CV Template" helps you visualize what it will actually look like. Chapter 8, "Getting Results from Your Portfolio," discusses how a portfolio can be a beneficial additional to your cover letter and résumé. Chapter 9, "Writing a Winning Cover Letter," explains the cover letter process in detail. Chapter 10, "Interview Realities," provides an overview of the entire interview process. Subsections include "Traditional and Behavioral Interviews" (two common methods employers use to interview candidates), "Sample Traditional and Behavioral Interview Questions," "Pre-Interview Questions," "Interview Myths Checklist," "Dressing for the Interview," "Ten Questions to Ask an Employer," and "Handling Inappropriate Questions."

I encourage you to take the time to do the hard work required to become your own job search expert. You have worked hard to earn your degree. I hope this book will motivate you to work even harder to tie your credentials to the real world of work. You will realize how good you are and acquire timeless knowledge that you can use throughout your lifetime. You have earned the opportunity to start your career—or to begin a new one.

Wishing you the best!

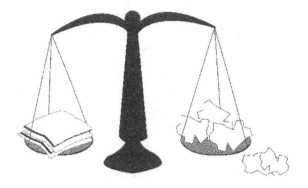

CHAPTER 1

HANDLING JOB SEARCH STRESS

Preparing and executing a job search can be stressful, depending upon your time restraints and current economic circumstances. Graduates often feel overwhelmed with the amount of work it takes to manage an employment search. However, you *can* take control of the process. It is important to view job hunt stress as an opportunity to put yourself in the employer's shoes.

Try to maintain a positive attitude by giving yourself credit for beginning your job search. The process is difficult and can leave you feeling frustrated. It involves time, research, and movement outside of your comfort zone. It challenges your status quo and may make life uncomfortable and confusing for a while. But the rewards will be worth your effort. Think about how some family members, friends, and acquaintances remain underemployed because they are afraid of the stress involved in planning a job search. If you learn how to recognize and manage your job search stressors, you can and will get hired.

Ten Job Search Stressors

Most college students experience job search stress. Sometimes it takes awhile before you realize how it affects your entire employment search. Once you identify areas of common stress other graduates experience, you will have the courage and motivation to keep moving forward. Approach the job search as you would an exam. When you have an exam to take, you research and study the topic to prepare yourself to answer all the questions. It's the same with job search stress—knowing ahead of time what can happen makes you stronger.

Job hunt stress is common. If it happens to you, it can have a devastating effect on your work and personal life. By learning how to identify your stressors you can navigate any job market successfully.

Feelings of discomfort and anxiety are strong indications of job hunt stress. They are warning signs of future job-related frustrations.

Mark "Y" for Yes, "N" for No, and "S" for Sometimes.

1. I feel anxious, confused, and fearful because I'm afraid I won't get hired. ____
2. I worry about opportunities for career advancement, and I feel I'll be lucky to get hired anywhere. ____
3. I'm afraid I'll have to accept a lower salary than I'd like just to pay off my college loans. ____
4. I'm unsure of myself because I believe other job seekers are more qualified. ____
5. I paid hundreds of dollars to have my résumé prepared, and it never generates interviews. ____
6. I feel vulnerable because I don't have all the qualifications the employer is asking for. ____
7. My stress level rises the minute I start my job search, because I'm not adequately prepared. ____
8. I'm afraid of the interview process. ____
9. I'm desperate to find a position I will love. ____
10. I'm afraid I won't get hired in my degree field. ____

Answers:

- *Three or more **yes*** answers to the questions above indicates you may be stressed out and need help and support. Searching for a job is difficult and filled with uncertainty. Asking for help is a positive approach to coping with your job search. Schedule an appointment with your college or university career services center and let him or her assist you with your entire job search.
- *Three or more **sometimes*** answers indicates you are beginning to understand how stressful a job search can be. Sometimes you may be unsure if you can handle the time-consuming task while preparing for graduation. It will be helpful to get extra support from your career services center.
- *A majority of **no** answers* indicates your doing a good job coping with job search stress. You're on the right track to getting hired.

Eight Job Search Strategies

Job search worries exist for most graduates. Learning how to handle them is challenging. Worries are a chance to learn more about yourself and cope with change. Review the Seven Strategies for Handing Job Search Worries and write them down on cue cards as a reminder of how you can overcome them.

1. **Develop Realistic Options**

Approach the job search with a multifaceted strategy, based on your career objectives and employer research. If you consider position opportunities from all angles, you can methodically develop a hiring action plan that works. In today's employment market, change is the name of the game. You have to be the leader of your own job search. Always have a job search plan A, B, and C. If you do, it is a strategy that will identify all potential career opportunities.

2. **Stay Focused**

Keep your eyes on the prize. Try to stay positive, even if (and when) you feel discouraged. See yourself getting hired by a great employer. Be patient, because it takes time and energy to stay focused on your job search goals. Find a mentor and be willing to ask for help from family and friends. Know that excellent positions are available in any job market.

3. **Go Easy/Adapt to Change**

Sometimes when graduates are in the beginning, middle, or end of a job search, it is easy to get frustrated. Maintaining a proactive, never-give-up attitude becomes difficult and stressful. If this happens to you, keep telling yourself you can do it if you go the extra mile. Never give up on yourself or your job search plan. You may have to modify it, change it, or even develop a new one, if the strategy isn't successful because of circumstances beyond your control. You will get hired if you keep adapting to change.

4. **Always Check Your Perceptions**

Inaccurate job search perceptions regarding the hiring process can impact your job search in many ways. It is not a guessing game where you hope you can win. If you don't have all the facts regarding the hiring process, from an employer's point of view, you may not get hired. It won't be because you're not the best candidate for the job. There may be other reasons. For example, it could be your cover letter, résumé, or interview skills that keep you back from getting offers. Please take time to find out what job strategies work best, based on accurate perceptions, while recognizing that there are exceptions to every rule.

5. **Depend on Yourself**

Take responsibility for your own job search. Yes, you may need help from your career services center, or from career development professionals. They can help you to sort through the hiring process. Remember, only you can measure and motivate yourself to follow through with a plan of action. This handbook helps you handle information overload. Know why you're the best graduate for the job. Prepare an excellent résumé and cover letter that stands out among the crowd. If your job search stalls, have the confidence to explore and find out the reasons why.

6. Release Fear

Job search fear can keep you from managing your time and talent. You have to market yourself to potential employers constantly and not take any job rejections personally. Have the courage to never give up until you make it through your job hunt transition, from college graduate to employee. Transitions always begin with an ending. For example, yours will be going from college graduate to professional in your career field.

7. Identify Your Unique Transferable Skills

Identifying your skills and transferable skills is a critical aspect of the job search process. These skills are the abilities employers look for in the workplace. Everyone has them, and they consist of natural and learned abilities. They are valuable because they are clues to the career field that suits you best. Matching them to specific occupational areas increases your employment marketability.

Many times graduates undervalue their transferable skills and define them within the narrow parameters of their current work experience. For example, if you are a teacher but want to make a career change into management, you may believe that all you can do is teach in the classroom. In reality, if you are an excellent teacher, you are organized, prepared, and creative with subject matter. Every day, you demonstrate your verbal and nonverbal communication skills with your students. Your leadership abilities are consistently on display with students, faculty, staff, and especially parents. The skills you use as a teacher can be easily transferred and applied to many fields in both the private and nonprofit sector, depending upon where your current interests lie. We can always define and redefine our skills and transferable skills. Keeping an open mind about constantly learning additional skills is a lifelong process.

If I asked you to identify your transferable skills, could you tell me what they are? If you can, your chances of getting hired increase significantly. If not, you have to focus on all your work experience, including internships, clinicals, and community service. Every experience contains a gold mine of clues to help you take ownership of your talents. You must know exactly what your transferable skills are. Employers want to hire employees who are confident about what they do. Imagine you are a manager or CEO of your own company or organization. What type of college graduate would you want to hire? Would your hiring decisions be based on academics only? Probably not! You would want to be sure the graduate you select is well rounded and has strong transferable skills prior to hiring. This will ensure that your investment in the candidate will benefit your company or organization.

8. Get Yourself Hired

It's important to approach your employment search with the same determination you used to earn your degree. Perhaps you struggled with a class or two, or perhaps you had to take a course over to raise your GPA. It's the same process. You had to develop a plan A, B, and C. You are a special graduate with credentials, special skills, and unique abilities, and your goal is to convince an employer to hire you. You have completed all your homework and are the best person for the job.

Swimming in the Goldfish Bowl

If you are graduating from college or are a recent grad, you don't want to be unemployed. You've worked hard for your education and want to find a great position. If you spend too much time stressing about your job search, you may begin to feel like a goldfish in a bowl, swimming around and around in circles. Your mind races: "What if the bowl shatters?" "How can I get a job?" "How can I cope with an uncertain employment market?" "What do I do?" Being in a goldfish bowl can be mind-boggling. What are your options? Sink or swim!

Of course, the goldfish bowl *does* offer some benefits. It provides temporary shelter from the reality of unemployment. It helps you feel safe and secure for short periods. This time-out can help you come to terms with a significant hiring transition. You might feel angry, scared, or uncertain. You might cry. Try to stay calm and patient even if your first impulse is to panic. Take comfort in the fact that what you're experiencing will only be temporary. The goldfish bowl can be your safety net. Your first reaction is to find something—*anything*—to be employed. It's wise, however, to take time to reflect and assess your situation before making a hasty decision. During this period of uncertainty, tap into your inner strength. Never give up on yourself. Realize your employment situation *will* change.

Visualize yourself being hired. What employment sector will you be working in? What will your life be like? Think about concrete ways to take charge of your career and find a position you will be happy with. View yourself as CEO of your own company: "Me, Inc." In today's world, employment security no longer exists. To remain marketable, you must be flexible and keep up with industry and workplace trends. Be prepared for failures along the way. View them as learning experiences.

Life is all about choices. As a college graduate, you may be entering the real world of work for the first time, or you may already have extensive work experience and want to change careers. No matter what your situation is, you have to begin your job search. The hiring transition process is unique. You have everything to gain and nothing to lose. Change is a lifelong companion. You can get hired if you try your best. You've earned your degree and are ready to enter your profession. Be proud of your accomplishments and work hard to get yourself hired!

The Meaning of Career Success

Career success means something different to each graduate. It's a lifelong process of discovering who you are and who you are becoming. It's the difference between contentment and frustration. It is the ability to balance your career and personal life. It is an ongoing process that changes throughout your lifetime. When you are beginning your career, it may take you awhile to gain enough work experience to move into your ideal position. It all depends on what your work and personal values are. For some individuals, earning a lot of money is a priority; for others, helping others is more important than a high salary. Perhaps you desire both. Try to avoid comparing your values to someone else's.

Values are important, because they will determine the employers you wish to work for and the positions you wish to hold. You may move from position to position before you find the perfect match. Often graduates will have to accept a position for a variety of reasons—for example, you need the money or the experience for a chance to gain additional skills. That's why it is critical to understand what your values are now. You want to find a position that will be a perfect match for your work values. Only you can measure your career success.

Please take the time to identify your top-priority values, because they will help you be happy in your career of choice. Career success means getting personal satisfaction out of your work life.

Exercise: Clarifying Values

Values clarification exercises help you identify your work-related values. In combination with your interests, they will help you identify your job goals. Review the results of your values clarification exercises. Use these values to prioritize the components you value in a career. Values are the key to discovering what is important and meaningful in your world of work. Your work-related values may change throughout your lifetime, but they remain the springboard for attaining a rewarding position. Try to look for your top three work-related values in positions you apply for, realizing that during uncertain economic times you may have to focus on your plan A, B, or C until your ideal position becomes available. For each answer, explain why following your answer.

1.   Do you value money, personal satisfaction, or both?

_____

_____

_____

_____

_____

2.   Do you like working independently or working with others?

_____

_____

_____

_____

_____

3.   Do you enjoy delegating or being a member of a team?

_____

_____

_____

_____

_____

4. Do you have excellent verbal and written communication skills and want to influence others?

_____

_____

_____

_____

5. Do you value your creativity and want to use it on a daily basis?

_____

_____

_____

_____

6. Would you prefer working in the private sector or in a community service environment based on your internships, volunteerism, or current work experience?

_____

_____

_____

_____

7. Do you value teaching or training others?

_____

_____

_____

_____

8. Do you want to work with the general public or a particular group of individuals?

_____

_____

_____

_____

9. Do you like working with numbers or balancing budgets?

_____

_____

_____

_____

_____

10. Do you want to be a problem solver or community activist?

_____

_____

_____

_____

_____

11. Do you want to be an advocate for others?

_____

_____

_____

_____

_____

12. What does the term respect mean to you in the work environment?

_____

_____

_____

_____

13. What type of supervisor do you want to work for?

_____

_____

_____

_____

14. What does the term success mean to you?

_____

_____

_____

_____

_____

15. What type of work environment do you want to work in? Structured? Unstructured? A combination of both?

_____

_____

_____

_____

16. What do you want your coworkers to be like? What personality type is your favorite?

_____

_____

_____

_____

_____

17. What style of leadership do you practice?

_____

_____

_____

_____

18. What work-related values do you respect the most?

_____

_____

_____

_____

19. Name three role models and explain why they are important to you.

_____

_____

_____

_____

_____

Review the results of your values clarification exercise. Were you surprised at the results? You have important values you can draw upon when searching for employment. Think carefully about the values you cherish most in the workplace. The values you select will benefit you in several ways. For example, if you value leadership opportunities but have selected an employer who limits training and personal development, you likely will not be happy in the position. If you like working directly with a variety of people every day but the position mainly requires you complete paperwork, you may become frustrated.

I can hear you saying, "How can I possibly know an employer's information before I apply for a position?" Knowing what your work values are will help you make good employment decisions. But the truth is that you may not be able to find a match strictly by researching an employer's values, mission, vision, or goals. This is a time when *who you know* can help. Tap into your network of contacts and see if you can receive feedback regarding your potential manager's/supervisor's professional reputation. However, neither you nor the employer will truly find out if you're a match until you're hired. Here is a personal example of what I mean.

I was already working and was recruited to apply for a higher level position. I applied and accepted the position without even trying to find out about my potential employer's management style. It didn't take long before I realized my supervisor was a micromanager with the entire staff. My personal satisfaction level and ability to work independently was almost nonexistent. I was stressed and frustrated because I had worked too hard to find a career I loved, only to end up with a supervisor with questionable leadership. I quit my job thinking I'd never be hired again. I took responsibility for my mistake. I had opportunities to do employer research, but I didn't take them. Now I am thankful that I was wrong, because I learned a lot about myself and the world of work. My credentials, internships, professional experience, and networking helped me find a rewarding position.

Employer research is an important step. If you can learn more about your future supervisor's management style, it's a plus. Each position you accept will help you find career satisfaction.

Remember, work values may change as time goes by and will be affected by changes in your personal life. Try to make sure your top three work-related values are reflected in all the positions you apply for. During uncertain economic times, you will have to make a job search plan that incorporates a plan B and C, until your ideal position becomes available.

Your Top Ten Work Values

(e.g., *training and education opportunities*)

1. _____
2. _____
3. _____
4. _____
5. _____
6. _____
7. _____
8. _____
9. _____
10. _____

Exercise: Your Strongest Skills

You may already know the skill areas you enjoy and excel in. The checklist below will help you identify the top priority skills you want to use or transfer into the workplace. Use this exercise as a guide to preparing additional skill sets and checklists unique to your own life experience.

What am I good at? For each entry below, provide specific examples of how you have demonstrated these skills.

1. Communicating with others

_____
_____
_____
_____

2. Listening

_____
_____
_____
_____

3.   Helping others

_____

_____

_____

_____

4.   Reading

_____

_____

_____

_____

5.   Being a team player

_____

_____

_____

_____

6.   Preparing reports

_____

_____

_____

_____

7.   Selling products

_____

_____

_____

_____

8.   Attention to detail

_____

_____

_____

_____

9. Working with numbers or balancing budgets

_____

_____

_____

_____

10. Working with the community

_____

_____

_____

_____

11. Advocating for others

_____

_____

_____

_____

12. Respecting others in the workplace

_____

_____

_____

_____

13. Motivating and inspiring others

_____

_____

_____

_____

14. Managing time

_____

_____

_____

_____

15. Solving problems

_____

_____

_____

_____

16. Being creative

_____

_____

_____

_____

17. Managing others

_____

_____

_____

_____

18. Working independently

_____

_____

_____

_____

19. Generating enthusiasm in others

_____

_____

_____

_____

20. Debating ideas

_____

_____

_____

_____

21. Teaching others

_____

_____

_____

_____

22. Doing technical work

_____

_____

_____

_____

23. Supervising others

_____

_____

_____

_____

24. Negotiating/arbitrating

_____

_____

_____

_____

25. Organizing/coordinating

_____

_____

_____

_____

Quick Tip

The above checklist represents only a fraction of the transferable skills each graduate has to offer. Prioritize your checklist to see if they are compatible with your interests. Put them aside until you complete the entire self-exploration process. Later, you will use them to zero in on the career field or positions you will apply for. Your marketability depends on them. They will help you gain the confidence to transfer within your career field and to look outside.

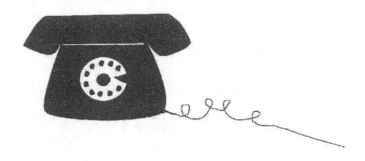

CHAPTER 2

NETWORKING COUNTS

N etworking is a reliable method of getting hired. Everyone you know, both inside and outside your chosen career field, can get you into the secret job market. This happens when you create a track record of professionalism.

For example, during your internships, clinicals, community service, volunteerism, or part- and full-time work experience, you have developed a network of people who can help you with employment leads. Alumni are also valuable assets in your network. Everyone you know has access to the hidden job market, the positions that become open before they are advertised.

If you let your network of contacts know the type of position you are looking for, they will put you on their to-do list. Networking is an interactive process that, if nurtured, will last a lifetime. You also have to be willing to help your contacts, because this will establish a track record of trust and mutual respect. Building formal and informal bridges of support ensures you will always become aware of career opportunities.

You must remember never to ask your contacts for a job, only for information. Always send a thank-you note for their time and helpful advice. Often your network of individuals will be able to provide you with a letter of reference, if it's applicable to the position you are applying for.

Networking Realities

1. **Networking is never out of style.**

Whether you are doing a job search or exploring additional career opportunities, networking is the most important method of connecting with the decision makers in your field of interest.

2. **Employers most often tap into their hidden network of contacts before going public with job openings.**

Activate or begin developing your network of personal contacts. They will provide you with valuable inside information regarding current or potential job openings. Your network will prove to be a good source of advice, suggestions, and feedback.

3. **Contact everyone you know who can be of assistance.**

Your network consists of individuals from both inside and outside your career sector. It includes family, friends, neighbors, past employers, and past coworkers. Even someone you meet causally may be able to provide you with an expanded network of contacts or open doors for you to have a "hands-on" learning experience. A network takes time to develop and nurture. There are no instant networks. Start building one now.

4. **The individuals you ask for help will only provide assistance if you have earned their respect.**

If you ask more of your contacts than they can or want to provide, you may find your career or job search shortchanged. Never ask someone in your network for a position; ask only for *information,* and share the fact that you are exploring career opportunities.

5. **Avoid the "Can I network with you?" approach with everyone you meet.**

If you only collect business cards or handshakes but never follow up and never help anyone else, you will not be establishing a network. You will never get beyond an introduction this way.

6. **Always let others know you appreciate their help and expertise.**

A productive network of contacts is cultivated for a lifetime. It allows you to navigate the world of work throughout your career. Each job search is unique, and who you know can open closed doors.

7. **You can increase your networking activities by volunteering, becoming involved in community service, working part-time jobs, and participating in internship, co-op, and shadowing opportunities.**

The bottom line of networking is to explore all your options by creating unique opportunities to learn about careers and job openings. Everyone knows someone who may be able to help you.

8. **Networking is the most productive career search and job hunt strategy.**

An active network is always in motion, in good and bad times. It's never too late to meet others. Networks provide a lifetime safety net, whether you are in the beginning, middle, or end of a job search. As a graduate and alumni of your college or university, contact former graduates, professors, administrative staff, and peers. Ask them for advice regarding your job search. The information they provide you will shorten your search.

Networking Homework

Developing a nurturing network of contacts takes time. Instant networks do not exist. To become an insider you must reach out and help others. You can even ask your contacts for letters of reference when you have established credibility with them.

List six ways your network of contacts can help you.

1. _____
2. _____
3. _____
4. _____
5. _____
6. _____

List six ways you can expand your network of contacts.

1. _____
2. _____
3. _____
4. _____
5. _____
6. _____

Will networking be a priority in your career and job search? If yes, explain the value of helping others.

_____
_____
_____
_____
_____

If not, explain the reasons why networking is a low priority.

_____
_____
_____
_____
_____

List three to five individuals you would like to have as networking mentors or role models.

Title _____

Employer/Company _____

Address _____

Telephone_____cell_____

E-mail address _____

Area of expertise_____

Reason why this person is a good contact _____

_____

Name_____

Title _____

Employer/Company _____

Address _____

Telephone_____cell_____

E-mail Address_____

Area of expertise_____

Reason why this person is a good contact _____

_____

Name_____

Title _____

Employer/Company _____

Address_____

Telephone_____cell_____

E-mail Address_____

Area of expertise_____

Reason why this person is a good contact _____

_____

Name_____

Title _____

Employer/Company _____

Address_____

Telephone_____cell_____

E-mail Address_____

Area of expertise_____

Reason why this person is a good contact _____

_____

Name_____
Title_____
Employer/Company_____
Address_____
Telephone_____cell_____
E-mail Address_____
Area of expertise_____
Reason why this person is a good contact_____
_____

Networking Tips

1. **Interview everyone who is doing what you want to do.**

Tap into your educational institution's alumni networking program of graduates who have volunteered to help you. Ask your family and friends if they know someone in your career field you can talk to obtain career-related information.

2. **Identify the person who does the hiring and ask for an opportunity to have a brief informational interview by telephone, or in person, to get career advice. Let them know how much you would appreciate their expertise.**

Send a cover letter, or call a company decision maker, and ask if you can schedule some time for a brief information interview. Be prepared with relevant questions.

3. **Widen your network of contacts by thinking out of the box and letting everyone know you are graduating.**

Think about who works in your career or related field. Who has inside information regarding new trends and hiring opportunities? List the most important contacts first. Then prepare a secondary list of potential contacts. Follow up on all levels with a call or cover letter, always thanking the individual. If they can't help you, ask if they can provide a referral to someone who can.

4. **Begin or continue to seek out others to gain work-related experience and networking opportunities.**

Always be on the lookout for a chance to gain more "hands-on" experience. Be open and willing to learn new skills.

5. **High visibility counts when you're in the middle of a job search.**

The above statement can't be repeated enough. Let everyone know you are looking for a position. Only don't become a pest. Try to work out a networking schedule. If you hear about an opportunity in casual conversations with acquaintances, share the fact you are doing a job search. It may turn into a valuable contact or referral.

6. Work hard to establish a proactive network.

You can't create a proactive network without developing positive relationships and favorable first impressions. Be aware of your verbal and nonverbal communication skills. For example, are you focusing on your soft skills, which include your ability to be a good listener? Are you a team player with collaboration and leadership skills? Do you consistently help others and have a global perspective? These skills will help you to develop an active network of contacts. Being assertive is also important, because it takes self-confidence to empower and encourage others to be their best. When you have volunteered your time, helped your peers, or demonstrated a strong work ethic, your contacts will respect you and help you to get hired.

7. Be willing to mentor and help others before and after you've been hired.

Be a great role model for others and be willing to share your expertise and experience. This is how you become a leader, who will always be on top of everyone's networking list.

8. Overcome your fear of asking for assistance. However, never specifically ask for a job, just information and advice.

Be brave and manage your fear. Keep it from holding you back from networking with others. You have more to lose by executing a job search all by yourself. Your network can provide you with tremendous support and encouragement.

9. Do your research when networking, and be specific with your contacts about how they can help you.

Always know exactly the kind of information you want from your contacts. They can usually provide you with the answers to your questions. They can lead you to job opportunities you can explore on your own.

10. Treat all contacts with respect and you will be advised of hidden career and job opportunities.

Be respectful and always thank your networking contact. Periodically keep in touch with them. Let them know how your career is going and how much you appreciated their help and advice. This is how you will stay at the top of people's minds.

Networking is easier said than done. If you are shy or assertive, you must carefully gain credibility with your contacts. The best way to do this is to concentrate on being a helpful individual with integrity. Demonstrate a desire to learn and help others. Always go the extra mile. Be cautious and willing to assist others. You can count on your contacts to provide you with valuable job search information if you are a team player.

Information-Gathering Interviewing

Information-gathering interviews are a great way to learn from professionals in your career field. They provide opportunities to create an informal network of contacts who can give you the facts regarding employment trends and job openings, as well as connect you with the decision makers.

Information-gathering interviews are invaluable. Interacting in person, by telephone, by e-mail, or by written correspondence with someone in your career (or a related field) can give you the inside track on what's happening in that field. Information-gathering interviews reveal current and potential job openings. They will also help you to gain confidence and increase your interviewing skills.

View each informational interview as an opportunity to make a good first impression. Ask only for information or for additional contacts, (e.g., if the contact is aware of a current or potential position opening). The contact will be willing to assist you only if she doesn't feel pressured to provide you with employment. Bring extra copies of your résumé to leave with every contact. It's the best way to get your résumé circulating.

Always send a thank-you letter within twenty-four hours of your informational interview. Let your contact know you appreciate their time and expertise. A hard-copy thank-you letter is often more appreciated, because it indicates you took the extra time to prepare and mail it. You can also buy a thank-you card and write a brief note of appreciation. Make sure all names and titles are spelled correctly. You also have the option of a thank-you e-mail. Use your judgment to decide which method will be beneficial.

Plan and prepare well in advance of your meeting. Know what specific information you are looking for and exactly how your contact can be of assistance. Have a plan prior to your first contact. Avoid "winging" the conversation and informational interview, and never ask your contact for a job. It is not the purpose of an informational interview.

The questions listed below will help to be well informed about the information-gathering interview process. Finding the answers to these questions will give you the confidence to continue the networking process and build a network of contacts that will allow you to tap into the hidden job market.

1. Can you tell me about future trends in my area of interest?
2. How long have you been in your field or position and what do you love about it?
3. Please share the challenges you have faced in your career and how you handled them.
4. May I schedule a convenient time to shadow you or another professional in your field?
5. Do you have any advice for me regarding gaining experience in my career field, or how to apply for a position?
6. Please tell me what skills and transferable skills are valued in my area of interest.
7. What personal characteristics do you look for when seeking a candidate for a position, internship, or volunteer opportunity?
8. Is there someone else with whom I can speak? Thank you for the great interview. I have learned so much from you. I'm trying to learn as much as I can about my career field. Do you know anyone else who might be willing to share their expertise with me?

Prepare an additional list of questions you would like answers to regarding current or potential job openings. Find out as much as you can about the nature of the position.

1. _____
_____
_____

2. _____
_____
_____

3. _____
_____
_____

4. _____
_____
_____

5. _____
_____
_____

6. _____
_____
_____

7. _____
_____
_____

8. _____
_____
_____

9. _____
_____
_____

10. _____
_____
_____

Quick Tip

Proper networking helps graduates become employment opportunity insiders. Please refer back to this chapter often. Always focus on helping others and your contacts will be there, providing you with information regarding current or potential job openings.

CHAPTER 3
THE JOB SEARCH PROCESS

The job search process involves making choices that affect both your professional and personal life. You fear selecting the wrong job target. These days, you will likely change jobs and career sectors multiple times. Employers want to hire employees who are dedicated and hard working, someone who offers the skills and transferable skills they are looking for.

Imagine the employment market as a thick rubber band being pulled in opposite directions. Imagine the stretching that occurs as career and job opportunities grow and expand. At any time the rubber band can snap back in the opposite direction. As a graduate, you must keep informed regarding occupational trends and projections. An excellent resource is the *US Government Occupational Outlook Handbook*. Please review the latest edition for employment trends, salaries, and projections. The document can be found online at http://www.bls.gov/oco.

Good employment search decisions involve compromise, commitment, and realistic goals. Your decisions should reflect your work and personal values. Matching your skills and interests to the workplace will help you set obtainable career and job goals. Your skills and interests will change over time, and you may decide to seek new employment opportunities that allow for professional growth.

Finding a position to match your talents involves trial and error and may include some failures along the way. The job search process begins when you identify your job target. You must stay focused and believe you are the best person for the job.

Ten Job Search Questions

The ten questions below pertain to the facts you need to complete your job search. Until you can answer all the questions, you will be limited in your potential to get hired. You must complete your employer research and select the best employer for your talents and experience. The questions will also help prepare you for the interview process and give you the tools to begin an effective job search.

1. a) Do I have accurate information about my potential employer, including
        mission statement, vision statement, and goals?
        Yes____ No__

    b) What do I still need to know?

Answer:

_____

_____

_____

_____

2. a) Have I used more than four resources for my employer research?
        Yes____ No__

    b) List resources below (e.g., The Occupational Outlook Handbook printed by the New York
        State Department of Labor:

    1. _____
    2. _____
    3. _____
    4. _____

3. Why am I the best person for the job?

Answer:

_____

_____

_____

_____

4. a) Have I talked with at least three individuals or alumni who work in similar positions?
Yes____ No____

   b) What have I learned about the job?

Answer:

_____

_____

_____

_____

5. a) Have I reviewed the latest issue of the US Department of Labor Occupational Outlook Handbook to review salary projections?
Yes____ No____

   b) What salary range am I willing to accept?

Answer:

_____

_____

_____

_____

6. How much do I want this job, and will I go the extra mile to get it? Please explain.

Answer:

_____

_____

_____

_____

7. a) If I can't get my ideal job, what is my second choice?

Answer:

_____

_____

_____

_____

   b) What are the titles and job responsibilities? (If possible, review an employer's organization charts, or review titles and responsibilities in the *US Department of Labor Occupational Outlook Handbook*.)

Answer:

_____

_____

_____

_____

8. a) Have I volunteered or completed an internship in my field of interest?
      Yes____ No____

   b) If so, list below. If not, identify three areas in which you would be interested in volunteering or doing an internship.

Answer:

_____

_____

_____

_____

9. a) Do I have a mentor who will help me with my job search?
    Yes___ No___

    b) If yes, list your mentor's name and title, and explain how he/she can help you. If no, list
    the names and titles of three potential mentors and explain how they can help you.

Answer:

_____

_____

_____

_____

10. List five reasons why the employer you selected should hire you.

    1._____
    2._____
    3._____
    4._____
    5._____

The purpose of preparing a detailed job search is to identify your skills and transferable skills. As a graduate, you must convince yourself that, regardless of your current employment situation, you are talented and capable. You can get the job you want if you focus on the employer's needs and your job qualifications. The critical aspect of a successful job search is attitude and perseverance. You must convince an employer—and yourself—that *you* are the best person for the job.

Job Search Survival Tips

- Great positions are always available in any job market.
- Develop a *revolving-door policy* by looking straight ahead and moving forward.
- Find a support network of positive people to encourage and guide you.
- Count on yourself. Only you know your definition of job success.
- Choose to give up old ideas and expectations and replace them with calculated risks.
- Keep learning about yourself. Attend workshops and seminars, cross-train, and increase your transferable skills.
- Understand what it means to network with others and learn how to become an insider.
- Tap into hobbies that can lead to job opportunities. For example, if you enjoy volunteering in your spare time, let your co-volunteers and supervisors know you are doing a job search.
- If you don't like your job, take a risk and change it! You have more to lose if you stay in a job you don't like.

Avoiding Pitfalls on the Web

Information is available online in a variety of ways. Job searchers need to be aware of the long-term results of their web presence. If you are a recent graduate who has a history of using MySpace or Facebook, be sure you clean up your profiles. All job searchers must be aware that their wall posts, blogs, group affiliations, and content on other websites may reveal unfavorable personal information about them or their friends.

Be cautious when you link to external websites. They often contain further links you may not be aware of, and your confidential data may no longer be yours. Always control the information others can see online. Only allow a select few to have access to your profile/websites.

You always want your online presence to be professional and above reproach. Whether you are applying for a paid position, internship, community service opportunity, co-op, clinical, volunteer, or shadowing experience, someone might check to see if your online activity reflects who you appear to be on your résumé or in an interview.

For example, an education graduate applied for a teaching position with an excellent school district. Her Facebook profile was checked by someone in the school district, including the postings on her wall. Many of the postings displayed inappropriate pictures and offensive language from her friends. The district felt that the applicant had poor judgment and never interviewed her. The candidate never found out the real reason why her application was rejected.

Employers are being cautious in the wake of nationwide reports of a decline in ethical decision-making. Most employers have tightened their employment requirements and want to hire qualified individuals with integrity and a strong work ethic. They want to make sure the person they hire is right for the long term. Hiring decisions are difficult, and making a poor choice costs every employer time, money, and credibility.

Your online presence must always be positive, not only for your job search but for your life as a whole. Consistently check to make sure it reflects the persona you wish to project.

Web Privacy Checklist

Use the Web Privacy Checklist to monitor your online presence. Your individual job search must include an online presence review. Information found on social network websites is often used by employers to get a picture of how the candidate presents him or herself in cyberspace. Please use the Web Privacy Checklist throughout your career. Even when you get hired and are established in your career, what you put online can get you fired. Here is an example of how someone can lose a leadership position. A recent graduate was hired by a community service employer and within the first two years became the president of their nonprofit board. Someone on the board, on their own, checked the new president's Internet presence and found pictures showing the individual drinking and partying with others. The board removed him from the position because they felt he was a poor role model for their organization.

The Web Privacy Checklist has been created for graduates who have never thought about how their online presence impacts their job search. The checklist gets you to think about how important it is to be professional online. If you check one or more *no* answers on the checklist, *your online persona may be undermining your job search.*

E-mail address	Identity protection	Personal websites	Online presence
1. Would you want an employer to view it? Yes____ No ____	1. Have you checked your Internet identity online? Yes _____ No _____	1. Are you on one or more social networking websites? Yes _____ No _____	1. Do you monitor what your friends post on your website? Yes ____ No _____
2. Is your e-mail address/addresses professional? Yes ____ No _____	2. Do you use the privacy settings to protect your identity? Yes _____ No _____	2. Do you care what others think about your online presence? Yes ____ No ____	2. Would an employer question your online credibility during an application process? Yes ____ No _____
3. Are you proud of your online presence? Yes ____ No _____	3. Do you know why it's important to check your online identity? Yes ____ No _____	3. Are your websites employer friendly? Yes _____ No _____	3. Would an employer fire you if they saw your online image? Yes ____ No _____
4. Does your e-mail address shock others or make them laugh? Yes ____No ____	4. Do you know how to protect your online identity? Yes _____ No _____	4. Would you worry if an employer or supervisor read your online profile? Yes _____ No _____	4. Do you keep your personal life private online? Yes ____ No _____
5. Have you reviewed your address/ addresses in the past 5 years to make sure it reflects who you are today? Yes _____ No ____	5. Have you checked the identities of others online? Yes _____ No _____	5. Have you reviewed your online identity recently? Yes _____ No _____	5. Do you know what would impress an employer online? Yes _____ No _____

This Web Privacy Checklist is a valuable tool that will help you to assess your Internet presence on social websites, by avoiding posting online pictures and activities that may include drug use, sexual activities, or bullying behavior. Everything you do on the Internet is a reflection of you. Please be careful and ensure your professionalism and integrity.

Job Search Schedule Template

The job search template is a practical goal-setting tool. Getting hired takes time, persistence, and a willingness to work hard every day. It will keep you focused and provide you the opportunity to monitor your progress.

Please use the job search template as an important goal-setting tool. Use it to monitor how you are moving forward in your employment search. Getting hired takes persistence and a willingness to keep up the pace. Your schedule will force you to stay focused on what you must do to be a competitive candidate. It allows you to measure your progress and tweak when necessary to ensure a successful job search.

Monthly / Weekly / Daily *To-Do* List

MONTH: _____

WEEK: _____

List two goals and decisions to be made.

Monday

1. _____

2. _____

Tuesday

1. _____

2. _____

Wednesday

1. _____

2. _____

Thursday

1. _____

2. _____

Friday

1. _____

2. _____

Saturday

1. _____

2. _____

Sunday

1. _____

2. _____

Daily and weekly accomplishments:

_____

_____

_____

Quiz: Would You Hire Yourself?

Write "Yes" or "No" after each question and explain why.

1. Can you give three of your qualifications for each job you are applying for?
    Yes___   No___

    My qualifications include:

    (1) _____
    (2) _____
    (3) _____

2. Will you be able to explain why the employer should hire you?
    Yes___   No___

    You should hire me because:

    _____
    _____
    _____

3. Are you confident about your ability to make a great first impression?
    Yes___   No___

    I am confident because:

    _____
    _____
    _____

4. Do you approach the job search from the employer's point of view?   Yes___ No___

    Please explain your answer:

    _____
    _____
    _____

5. Did you research each potential employer?
    Yes___   No___

    What did you do?

    _____
    _____
    _____

6. If you were the employer, would you hire yourself?
    Yes____   No____

Why would you hire yourself?

_____

_____

_____

7. Have you determined what your salary qualifications are?
    Yes____   No____

What are they? How will you approach the question?

_____

_____

_____

8. Are you prepared to dress for the interview and not the job?
    Yes____   No____

My professional interviewing outfit includes:

_____

_____

_____

9. Can you give three examples of your job-related achievements?
    Yes____   No____

    Achievements:

    (1) _____
    (2) _____
    (3) _____

If you answered *yes* to 1 through 9 you are going to have a successful job search! You will get hired or be given a chance to become a finalist.

If you answered *yes* to 7 or 8 questions, your chances of getting the job offer are iffy. Immediately review the entire quiz. Begin research on yourself and potential employers at once.

If you answered *yes* to fewer than 7, you must spend more time on your entire job search process.

Quick Tip

The job search process provides a realistic framework for getting hired. If you use all the suggestions in this chapter, you will increase your chances of getting on top of the hiring list. Knowing as much as you can about yourself and a potential employer increases your confidence and ability to prepare an assertive job search. You can and will get hired if you work as hard as you did to graduate. You can do it!

CHAPTER 4
MARKETING YOUR QUALIFICATIONS

Résumés 101

Have you ever been influenced by television commercials? Do they sometimes get your attention in negative ways? Do you ever switch channels when they come on or find yourself tuning them out? When you are impressed with a commercial, do you often go out and buy the product? Is there a commercial that always makes you smile? Think about how you react to them. They only get a few seconds to make a first impression. It is the same with your résumé. It is a commercial about your qualifications in your career field.

How you present yourself in print or online has a major impact on an employer's reaction to your qualifications. All graduates need a résumé worthy of a positive first impression. Your document provides employers with a method for screening candidates for current or future job openings. Your résumé will either help or hinder your job search.

There are many résumé formats you can choose from. You want to select the one that highlights your work history and skills in the most favorable way. Detailed information regarding the résumé process is available in chapters 5, 6, 7, and 8.

If you send your résumé out randomly to employers, without doing your research or obtaining a contact's name, you will leave an employer shaking his or her head. It will be obvious to that person that you didn't do your homework. Always put yourself in the employer's shoes. What kind of employee would you be looking for? If you received hundreds of résumés from graduates who obviously didn't understand the value of first impressions, you would likely only focus on the candidates who did.

You can do it! You can be the graduate who gets an interview.

All college graduates need a résumé or CV, because it provides employers with an easy method to screen for potential openings.

Nearly everyone who has written a résumé considers him or herself an *expert*. The list includes family, friends, neighbors, peers, employment specialists, career counselors, and professional résumé preparers. Many of these people may have told you the following:

- "My résumé worked for me; you can just change a few words."
- "Just handwrite your résumé. It won't matter."
- "Be real … a résumé is just a résumé … no big deal."
- "Just tell them what they want to hear."
- "All résumés are the same."
- "An outline will do. It's easy."
- "My way is the only way to do it."
- "I just read a book that says …"
- "A professional prepared my résumé for me, and it cost over $200. It must be good."
- "Use a computer program template. It's easy."

Always consider the pros and cons of such *expert* suggestions and make your own decisions regarding your résumé content. **Never underestimate your own ability to construct a distinctive résumé.**

Curriculum Vitae 101

A curriculum vitae is an extended version of your résumé. The same résumé marketing advice applies. However, you now have the flexibility to add as many additional pages as you need to highlight all your experience, skills, and academic achievements.

The CV is a document commonly used when you have a doctorial or professional degree. It is an extended version of a résumé and can be as long as necessary to provide a detailed description of your academic and professional achievements. See Chapter 7 for a CV template.

Résumé/CV Advice

- Know why you are the best person for the job and prove it. For example, study the qualifications for the position carefully. Usually they are listed in priority order. Be sure to incorporate the transferable skills they are looking for, using examples from your work or work related experiences.
- Research potential employers and ask professionals in the field for information and advice on what they look for in a résumé.
- Understand the purpose of a résumé/CV and how it reflects your background and skills.
- Approach the résumé/CV writing process from the employer's point of view, and stay focused on the qualifications of the position opening.
- Prove you are the best candidate, with specific examples and action verbs.
- Ask for guidance and advice from several reliable sources, including future employers.

- Realize the same résumé/CV format may not work for everyone.
- Find a résumé buddy, mentor, or coach, and ask for an honest evaluation of your résumé/CV content.
- Review several formats before you select the one that's right for you.
- Always question the experts before you hire someone to help you. Make sure you ask if their job seekers have successfully found positions in a reasonable period after they have provided assistance. Also ask for references from clients.

Questions for Job Search Experts

Graduates must be educated job hunters. Always ask the job search experts questions regarding their success rates before hiring them to help you with your résumé or job search.

1. Are you knowledgeable regarding my job target. If so, how can you prove it? Have your clients received opportunities to interview for position openings? Please explain.

_____

_____

_____

_____

_____

2. Have you helped someone with a similar job search within the last year? If yes, for what position and how does this relate to the position I want to apply for? Please explain.

_____

_____

_____

_____

_____

3. Please provide me with three references from successful job hunters.

a. _____

b. _____

c. _____

Foolproof Résumés/CVs

A college graduate's worst nightmare is the fear that his or her résumé/CV will end up in the wastepaper basket—the final resting place for discarded documents that stand out for all the wrong reasons. If your CV is fragmented and disorganized, it also sends a signal to the employer that the graduate who created it, namely, that this person doesn't have a clue about the responsibilities that come with the position. If your résumé/CV contains only fragments of your job history and lacks a description of your transferable skills related to the position opening, it will be overlooked.

The best way to stand out among the crowd is to craft an individualized résumé/CV. Never, ever exaggerate your credentials or work history, because it's dishonest and will ruin your chances of getting hired if you are found out. If you prepare an ordinary résumé/CV that is unassuming and boring, it will be ineffective. An employer is looking for someone who is unique, qualified, and a perfect match on paper.

- Your individualized résumé/CV is an opportunity to provide excellent examples of your qualifications, skills, and experience.
- Your confidence and pride must shine through the text.
- The document establishes a clear connection to the job description.
- Your résumé/CV highlights your writing ability and attention to detail.
- It should clearly target your achievements and ability to meet specific job qualifications.
- It opens doors and creates opportunities to showcase your individuality.
- You can prove credibility on paper and gain an interview opportunity.
- It prepares you for the interview process.
- It accurately documents your employment history.

Employers differ in what they look for in a résumé/CV. For that reason, it's important to do your research and make it unique. Always remember that there are exceptions to every single rule. The length of your résumé depends on your individual skills and qualifications. If you decide to stretch the truth, chances are you will expose yourself during the prescreening or interview process. Your document is a written handshake that reaches the employer before your do. You want to create a foolproof document you can be proud of.

Individually crafted résumés/CVs have text that is clear, concise, and accurate, and meets most or all the position requirements. It also contains lots of white space between headings. There are no exaggerations or inaccuracies. Your résumé is unique and creative and unlike everyone else's.

In a foolproof document, your work experience is a "word-for-word" description of your past or current job responsibilities. Employers, however, want to know what *you* do, not simply what you *have done*. They are rarely interested in references prior to the interview and like to have them upon request, separate from your résumé.

Employers want you to demonstrate, in your own words, how organized and accurate you are. Your résumé/CV will generate interviews if it contains strong content, not fluff. It must be prepared with tender, loving care. You have worked hard to earn your degree, and now you have an opportunity to prove to an employer how good you are.

Eight Foolproof Tips

1. All your past and current job experiences, paid or unpaid, are relevant.
2. The length of your résumé/CV depends on your individual skills and experience. The document can be from one to three pages if the content is strong and focused on your career goal.

3. Your document must be proofed for typos and errors. Do not rely on spell check only.

4. Consider writing a detailed profile on your résumé/CV as an attention getter, targeted to the position you are applying for. For example, if you are a business graduate and are applying for a position as an administrative assistant in an accounting firm, you could say "Diligent business graduate with administrative internship experience in government sector. An experienced team player who will work hard to achieve an employer's goals and objectives."

5. Always research your target employer and never *"wing it."* Employers will usually discover if you have, during your interview.

6. Take your time writing and rewriting your final draft.

7. Make sure your résumé/CV is easy to read and understand. Use action verbs within your descriptions. For example, if you are a liberal arts graduate applying for an editorial assistant position, you could say something like, "Edited campus newspaper monthly and coordinated all activities leading to publication."

8. An excellent résumé/CV is a snapshot, a ten-second commercial, and a confidence booster that gives a potential employer a guided tour of your work experience.

Résumé/CV Research

Writing the most effective résumé/CV possible can be confusing and stressful. The job market in the twenty-first century will sometimes be challenging. You are a business of one and will have to keep learning about what's happening in your career field. You must be an innovative team player and demonstrate leadership skills. Your résumé/CV must reflect how responsible and reliable you are. The descriptions you use must be specific and include transferable skills.

It is necessary to prepare a backup job search plan that includes additional career options. For example, suppose your plan A is to graduate and find a position in your career field. If you have studied teaching, you want to teach. If you have studied nursing, you want to work in a specific health-care environment. If you find you are having a hard time getting hired because of current economic conditions, you will have to pursue plan B, which will be related to your plan A objective.

For example, if your specialized certification area is in Elementary Education and teaching positions are hard to find because of uncertain economic times, you can still apply for positions in a nonprofit organization or private business sector, where all your teaching skills are transferable. If you are a nurse and can't work in a hospital because of a hiring freeze, your plan B may be to work for an HMO, nursing home, or business. Your plan C may be to work in the insurance industry, or in a legal setting.

As a graduate you will have to be flexible and constantly aware of changes in your career field. When the job market is tough you need to work on all three plans at the same time. If positions are abundant you can still keep your plan B and C prepared and ready to go, in case you need to implement them.

There are four basic steps to creating a terrific résumé/CV. Use the following steps to take control of your job search.

STEP I: Choose at least three specific job targets, including titles and employers.

Target 1:

_____

_____

_____

_____

_____

Target 2:

_____

_____

_____

_____

_____

Target 3:

_____

_____

_____

_____

_____

- Research each potential employer. Include information on their mission, vision, and goals.

Employer 1

Mission:

_____

_____

_____

Vision:

_____

_____

_____

Goals:

_____

_____

_____

Employer 2

Mission:

_____

_____

_____

Vision:

_____

_____

_____

Goals:

_____

_____

_____

Employer 3

Mission:

_____

_____

_____

Vision:

_____

_____

_____

Goals:

_____

_____

_____

STEP II: Imagine you have a specific job opening to fill and you want to hire the best candidate. What are the required skills and qualifications? Make a detailed list and use it as a guideline when building your résumé.

Employer 1

Skills:

_____

_____

_____

Qualifications:

_____

_____

_____

Employer 2

Skills:

_____

_____

_____

Qualifications:

_____

_____

_____

Employer 3

Skills:

_____

_____

_____

Qualifications:

_____

_____

_____

STEP III: Again, picturing yourself as the employer, what important facts have you learned?

Employer 1

_____

_____

_____

_____

_____

_____

Employer 2

_____

_____

_____

_____

_____

_____

Employer 3

_____

_____

_____

_____

_____

_____

STEP IV: Review a variety of books on building résumés, checking both copyright dates and the credentials of the author.

Which résumé books or websites have you selected to gather résumé format information from?

_____

_____

_____

_____

_____

_____

Quick Tip

Marketing your qualifications successfully takes time and perseverance. Keep going the extra mile to ensure your résumé/CV will get noticed by employers. You can do it if you try! Someday you will be the employer searching for candidates for new positions. Approaching the job search form an employer's point of view will help you to make a positive first impression.

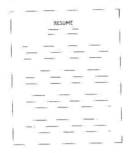

CHAPTER 5
RÉSUMÉ/CV BASICS

This chapter will provide you with a detailed outline of the required and optional information you will need in your résumé/CV. In the section "CV Highlights," we will address the differences between the résumé and the CV.

Required Information

The following information is required for both a résumé and a CV. The goal is to analyze your entire work history, focusing on your valuable skills and transferable skills.

Self-Identification

Always include your name, address, zip code, telephone number, and e-mail address. Include a temporary address if necessary.

Be sure to avoid using nicknames and unprofessional e-mail addresses. The recorded message on your answering machine must also be professional. For example, *"I'm currently unavailable; please leave your name, number, and a brief message, and I will return your call as soon as possible"* would be appropriate. When an employer calls and your message machine plays your favorite dance music and you say, "I'm in the middle of a party, I'll catch up with you later," the caller may move into the next candidate leaving no message. Over the years employers have complained about some candidates' poor telephone etiquette. "Hey, what's up?" is not the most professional greeting, and nor is "I'm having a bad day. Call back" (both real-life cases). Throughout your entire job search, you want to present a good first impression. Pretend you're the employer and act accordingly.

Education

If you have graduated within the last one or two years, list your education information prior to your work experience. If it has been more than two years since graduation, enter the information after your relevant work experience. If you have recently returned to college for an advanced degree, include your education prior to your work experience. If you are attending college for the first time, place it on your résumé prior to work experience.

Your education history includes all degrees, majors, names of schools, cities and states (do not include street addresses or zip codes of colleges), and year of graduation or anticipated month and year of graduation. Grade point average can be included if you earned a 3.0 or higher. If you attended a college or university and earned credits but no degree, you can include that information under your education heading, listing coursework completed in addition to the college name, city, state, and years attended.

Work Experience

This heading includes several optional subtitles. The headings you choose should reflect your professional life and relevant activities. For example, you may choose a heading titled *Professional, Management, Clinical, Internship,* or *Leadership Experience.* The title selected should reflect your career field and job target.

Everyone is unique. You can use a variety of the above headings, or create new ones, to reflect your relevant work experience. List each job heading first, followed by position title, name of employer, city and state, and dates or years of employment. If you have worked with one employer for a long time, you can stress your transferable skills and accomplishments. If you have worked for an employer for a year or less, describe your experience in terms of skill-based knowledge, focusing on your soft skills, including interpersonal skills (both written and verbal), collaboration, flexibility, team building, and leadership experience.

Quick Tip

Your professional document is a reflection of who you are at this moment in your career. Take into consideration your special interests, skills, and accomplishments in addition to your education and work experience.

Optional Information

Job or Career Objective

You may state an objective when you have a particular position in mind. Your objective can simply list a position title—for example, Elementary Teacher, Physical Therapist, Nurse Administrator, Physician Assistant, or Librarian. If you use only the title of the position you are applying for, you can expand on your objective in your cover letter.

You can choose to expand on your Job or Career Objective within this heading. Do so by including one or several statements identifying your specific objective.

Avoid using a generic job objective (e.g., *Seeking an administrative position in health care where I can utilize my excellent communication skills as well as my organizational and leadership experience*). Why is the above statement generic? Anyone can say they have *great communication, organizational, and leadership experience*. To be more effective, demonstrate these skills by writing a *specific* statement regarding your success in these areas. Be brief and to the point—for example, *Experienced Health Care Administrator seeking to work in an assisted living environment with opportunities to streamline costs and expenditures while meeting an employer's organizational goals and objectives.*

Quick Tip

Always be brief and to the point when writing an objective. The objective must target your job goal. Hook the employer with your words and descriptions. You can also choose to omit it entirely and refer to your objective in your cover letter only.

Résumé Summary

A résumé summary is similar to a job or career objective, except that it is used to highlight only work-related experience and education. For example, if you are applying for the position of Program Director for a community service agency and your management experience is in the private sector, your goal in the summary will be to demonstrate how your skills transfer to the nonprofit sector.

Sample Résumé Summary

Hardworking Program Director with excellent business experience and extensive community service. Dedicated professional and client advocate seeking a management position in the nonprofit sector.

Profile

The résumé profile is targeted toward a specific position opening. It differs from a Job or Career Objective or Résumé Summary by providing detailed information; it also matches the skills and qualifications an employer is looking for. It must generate attention. Every word must count, relating to the potential or current opening.

Sample Profile

Experienced Marketing Director with ten years leadership experience managing a successful team of professionals. Seeking to transition into the nonprofit sector to help an organization meet their community-based goals and objectives.

Qualifications Brief

A qualifications brief is used to highlight soft skills, such as communication skills, team building, problem solving, and leadership abilities. It is useful when changing positions within your employment field. It can be used to demonstrate specialized experience. Be sure that it focuses on accomplishments and achievements relevant to the position you are applying for.

Sample Qualifications Brief

Registered Nurse with extensive experience caring for underserved populations.
Taught college-level wellness courses to freshman and sophomore nursing students.
Advocated for single parents, teens, children, and the well-elderly.
Administered successful wellness grant program for a public university population.

Quick Tip

The qualifications brief must be focused, specific, and targeted to the requirements of the position.

Philosophy Statement

A philosophy statement can be used to describe your personal view of your profession. It is a statement based on truth and must avoid exaggerations, and it is especially useful in the healthcare, medical, teaching, and educational fields, although it can be applied to all occupations. It can be crafted in various ways. You must be creative and get the reader's attention immediately.

Sample Philosophy Statement

Diligent health services professional who believes each individual deserves to be treated with respect, compassion, and dignity, in the tradition of both Western and holistic medicine.

Quick Tip

You also have the option of not using any of the above headings, instead targeting your objective in your cover letter.

Transferable Skills

Use this heading if you want to stress your strongest areas of expertise. Many skill sets are transferable to a variety of positions. For example, if you have proven leadership, communication, written, and organizational skills, you can transfer these skills to an occupation where they are required. Prove that you have the required experience by giving specific examples of what you've accomplished inside and outside your field. Employers want to hire employees who are well-rounded individuals with diverse talents.

Quick Tip

Always avoid the use of the words I and my on your résumé. This helps graduates focus on actual position qualifications. From an employer's perspective, this practice often proves successful (although there are exceptions to every rule).

Work-Related Experience

Use this heading on your résumé if the work is relevant to your job or career objective. Include it under the work experience heading or in addition to it. List title, name of employer, city and state, and dates employed. This optional heading can include volunteer work, community service, internships or service learning, clinicals, co-ops, and part-time jobs.

Quick Tip

All work experience is valuable to an employer, regardless of whether you were paid. Never underestimate the value of your experiences outside your career field; they give you an advantage in the hiring process.

CV Highlights

CVs are different from résumés, as they highlight your doctoral or professional degree areas. You must organize your CV by prioritizing your optional headings. Focus on the skills that your potential employer values. Show your grasp of the responsibilities of the position you are applying for. Always lead with your highest level of experience. (Review all of chapter 5.) Be creative and detailed, and make every word count. You are not limited by the number of pages in your CV, as long as it provides an accurate picture of you as an ideal candidate.

Quick Tip

You have worked hard to earn your academic credentials. Never short change yourself. Give yourself credit for all your unique talents, skills, and work history. Let your CV be a masterpiece of your viability as an outstanding candidate.

Optional Headings

Use optional headings to highlight and strengthen your résumé/CV. They help give an employer insight into your unique background and experience. Optional headings are as individual as you are, and only you can decide which ones are relevant to your current career goals. You may even create new headings if necessary.

Accomplishments/Achievements – List special activities or events in your life you are proud of. They can be work or community related.

Athletics/Athletic Leadership – List participation in athletics or being a coach or assistant coach indicates your ability to be a both a team player and a leader.

Awards/Scholarships – Use one or more headings, as appropriate. Include relevant information and dates.

Campus Involvement – Use this heading if your activities are related or transferable to your job target. Good examples include experiences within the last five years.

Certifications – Use one or more headings, as appropriate. Include relevant information and dates.

Clinicals – List highest-level clinical first and describe as you would actual work experience.

Computer Software/Technology/Web Design – List the names of the computer programs at which you are proficient (e.g., Excel, Word, Photoshop, or website design projects).

Community Service – Use this heading if your activities are related or transferable to your job target. Good examples include experiences within the last five years.

Cooperative Education – List any job experiences earned in conjunction with academic credit. This heading should be considered as important as paid work experience.

Honors – Use one or more headings, as appropriate. Include relevant information and dates.

International Community Service – Include volunteerism served internationally.

International Experience – List work you have done or are doing internationally.

Internships – Include any on-the-job training experiences. This heading should be considered as important as paid work experience.

Languages – Use only if you are fluent or conversational in a second language.

Leadership – This heading can be used to highlight paid or unpaid accomplishments and achievements where you have demonstrated leadership qualities.

Licensures – Use one or more headings, as appropriate. Include relevant information and dates.

Mentoring – Use if you have had opportunities to help others increase and gain confidence or specialized skills in their areas of interest.

National Community Service – List all special volunteer projects throughout your native country.

Practicum – Include the number of hours worked in your on-the-job training.

Professional Development – Include meetings, seminars, or career-related experiences.

Professional Organizations/Memberships/Affiliations – List only organizations/ affiliations that apply to your job target.

Publications – Include relevant research and published material. Recent graduates may include the title of their thesis/research project.

Research Projects – Include relevant research and published material. Recent graduates may include the title of their thesis/research project.

Service Learning – Include projects that are academically related.

Special Interests – Include a reference to your special interests only if they relate to your job target, or if they provide a background to your career field.

Specialized Research – List research related to your career field or doctoral project.

Thesis – Include relevant research and published material. Recent graduates may include the title of their thesis/research project.

Volunteerism – Use this optional heading if your activities are related or transferable to your job target. Good examples include experiences within the last five years.

Quick Tip

Do not list date of birth, marital status, height, weight, and controversial memberships on your résumé. This information may screen you out of an interview. It may also bias an employer against you due to personal preferences. Your main objective is to gain an interview based on your education skills, which you have already acquired, and your proven ability to learn new skills and work-related talents. Personal information is confidential and must be omitted from your résumé. **Never include your driver's license or social security number because of the potential for identity theft.**

CHAPTER 6
HOW TO PREPARE YOUR RÉSUMÉ/CV

Organizing Your Résumé/CV

Beginning a résumé or CV is like preparing for graduation. You need to make sure you complete all the required coursework before you can graduate. If you don't study and pass your exams, you will be unable to walk across the stage to receive your diploma. When you write a résumé or CV, you have to make sure you complete all your job search homework. Then you can select a format that highlights your career experience. You have to keep your eye on the prize. Your goal is to get hired as soon as possible.

This chapter contains an overview of the three basic formats that you can adapt and change to give you the framework you need to begin the process. The basic résumé worksheet and optional headings also apply to CVs. A CV is an extension of a résumé. By reviewing all the résumé information, you will be able to organize a unique CV.

There are three basic résumé (and CV) formats to choose from: chronological, functional, and targeted. There are many variations of each format. You must be creative and prepare an individualized résumé designed to highlight your unique talents and skills.

Chronological Résumé/CV

Within this format, your work experience is listed in chronological order, beginning with your most recent work history. Titles and organizations are emphasized. Skills, achievements, and accomplishments within these titles are described in detail.

Advantage
The chronological format highlights your career growth and your strong work ethic. The résumé/CV is easy to follow. All paid or unpaid work is presented. It shows growth and focuses on your education, skills, transferable skills, and achievements.

When to use
Use a chronological résumé/CV when your job target is directly related to your work history, or when the name of your last employer adds strength to your résumé. A chronological résumé can be used by almost everyone to demonstrate what you have accomplished to date. Whether you are a first time graduate, or career changer returning to work, or retiree starting a new career, it gives an employer a snapshot of your relevant skills and interests.

Quick Tip

Your experience can go back ten years or more if your past employment is relevant to your current job target. If you are a recent graduate, you can focus on your work-related experience, internships, volunteerism, and campus involvement.

Functional Résumé/CV

The functional résumé/CV focuses on major areas of achievements and strengths. This résumé format allows you to organize your work history in a way that supports your job objective. For example, if you are applying for a marketing coordinator position and have won the Marketing Intern of the Year Award for a local nonprofit organization, you could include it as a subcategory under marketing experience. It could be titled "Achievements." The major headings you select reflect your skills and transferable skills in relation to the requirements of the job for which you are now applying. Examples of optional headings include Management/Organizational Skills, Leadership Experience, and Communication/Public Relations Skills. You can list your actual titles and work history below your major headings.

Advantage
The functional résumé/CV allows for flexibility when applying for a variety of job targets. You can be creative with job descriptions. It helps you show an employer exactly how your employment history relates to your current job target. The focus is on skills and transferable skills.

For example, you have demonstrated excellent soft skills, including leadership, team building, and collaboration in an unrelated position, and you can give accurate examples of how your skills can be transferred into another job target. Your functional résumé can focus on your transferable skills sets by showing an employer how they apply to their position opening.

When to use

The functional résumé/CV is used when you're changing career fields, doing a new job search, or reentering the job market. It is an opportunity to prove you have the qualifications and skills the employer is looking for. It must contain specific descriptive statements and be focused on the position requirements. To do this, you have to complete your employer research and know exactly the type of candidate the complier is looking for. When describing your work or work-related experience, you have to give examples within your descriptions. This will encourage an employer to interview you for the opening.

Quick Tip

If you have worked for an employer for a year or more, reference the year only. If less than a year, note the dates in months.

Targeted Résumé/CV

This format can be used for a specific job target and is similar to the functional format, only it isn't as flexible. You also have to know what the position requirements are. You are applying for a specific position and will modify your document for each opening. However, in order to write one, you must know exactly what skills set the employer is looking for.

Advantage

The targeted format is less flexible than the functional résumé because it's geared toward one specific position. It is used often when you are applying within your field of expertise.

When to use

Use a targeted résumé/CV when job titles do not reflect your job experience. A targeted résumé shows potential employers exactly why you're qualified for their position opening.

Quick Tip

A targeted résumé/CV must clearly show a relationship between your experience and job target. It will be different for each job target.

To begin organizing your résumé/CV, you must first research your job target thoroughly. Then you should review your entire employment history and the requirements of the position you are applying for. Use the Basic Résumé Worksheets to choose the correct titles and structure of your résumé/CV. Be creative and design an individualized document highlighting your special talents and skills. Only you can decide which format is best for you.

Résumé/CV Dos and Don'ts

Please use Résumé/CV Dos and Don'ts as a guide and reality check. Always remember, each employer is unique and there are exceptions to every rule.

- Your résumé/CV must look professional and be printed on quality bond paper (**never** use copy paper). White, light gray, tan, and beige are good color options. Applicants in creative career fields (e.g., graphic design, advertising) can be more artistic in their choice of color. Use either a standard business envelope of the same paper or a manila envelope to mail. Type the address and return address. Do not staple your résumé/CV. You have as little as ten seconds to create a winning first impression. The use of professional-looking paper and envelopes will give you a leading edge.
- Your résumé should be one page long, more if it contains substance—never add fluff. Include your name and the page number on succeeding pages to prevent your résumé from being misplaced. Your CV can be as many pages as necessary if you have extensive academic credentials and experience.
- Do not number page one; number consecutive pages only.
- Headings and dates should be easy to read.
- Insert a double space between each heading.
- Use 12-point font for your text and 14-point bold for your major headings.
- Always be truthful on your document and do not embellish.

Only you can decide if a one-, two-, or three-page résumé is appropriate. The determining factor will be the *substance* of the information you include. For a résumé, it is better to have one page that is content rich than two pages that include unnecessary information. Every word must count. Show rather than tell the employer why you are a good candidate. A Curriculum Vitae is an exception to this rule. It can be as long as necessary, because it contains extensive documentation of your professional experience and academic credentials. For example, if you have been responsible for co-organizing an outreach alumni advisory council, you can say, "Co-created and organized a successful alumni advisory council to encourage current and future graduates to become active alumni members."

Quick Tip

Ready ... get set ... go! You'll need plenty time, patience, and the desire to craft a quality résumé/CV. Do not compare your document to anyone else's. You are one of a kind. You have the ability to go the extra mile, using accurate, specific, descriptions of your educational and career related achievements.

Online Résumé/CV Basics

There are many ways to submit your résumé/CV online to thousands of websites. You will have a variety of options. For example, you can upload it or copy and paste it online, according to each site's directions.

To ensure your online submission will be easily scanned into most employers' computer systems, review all the guidelines in this handbook, mainly because all the key words will already be included on your document. Read the employer's submission protocol carefully. Each site's directions will be different.

Although each employer will have a different protocol regarding their submission process, you must carefully read each site's directions to ensure your résumé/CV doesn't get lost in cyberspace.

Submit online and send a hard copy directly to an employer if possible. If you only post it online, you limit your potential to get hired. It is often hard to follow up with an online submission, because they are screened by a computer rather than an individual.

You can successfully submit online if your qualifications are an exact match.

A word of caution. When submitting your résumé/CV online, be careful. Even popular job boards such as Monster.com have been scammed by bogus employers using their system. They do it to mine for personal information, which can be used unethically. You are safe if you apply directly to a reputable company or organization's website.

Always read the privacy policies regarding all your online submissions. Here are two examples of what can happen if you are not observant.

A physical therapy graduate was applying for positions online when she received an immediate employment offer from an out-of-state employer. Fortunately, she called the career services center, asking for advice. Her family was concerned, because the employer immediately asked her for her social security number. When asked if the graduate had researched the employer, she answered that she had not. All she did was to read the information on their website. Needless to say, she immediately stopped all correspondence and reported the bogus employer to the site's webmaster.

A recent business graduate was applying for an accounting position from out of state when he received an offer. They too wanted extensive personal information. He had worked on his résumé extensively and was excited about how good it was. However, something about their offer didn't feel right. He also called the career services center asking for advice. I suggested he call the local Better Business Bureau to check on their legitimacy. The graduate received a negative report from the Better Business Bureau within the state where the job was supposedly located. The information saved him from accepting a nonexistent position.

There are also many success stories from graduates who applied and accepted excellent positions posted online. Your hard copy document can easily be revised for an online submission and incorporated to apply to each employers requirements.

- List your name, telephone number, and e-mail address on separate lines as a header on your résumé.
- Your computer résumé/CV will be selected based on how many keywords the search engine finds based on the employers job description.
- Print the résumé/CV on quality bond paper.
- Computerized résumés can be longer than traditional résumés.
- Automated computer systems scan résumés/CVs for more than one position at a time and may increase your interviewing opportunities.

Quick Tip ───────────────────────────────

Your hard-copy document can easily be used to generate your computer résumé. Use the same major headings and key skill words to describe your work experience. Do not italicize, underline, or use bullet points on a computer résumé.

Basic Résumé/CV Worksheets

Please be aware that you will not be including all résumé/CV elements. You have to determine what is necessary to include, based on your special skills and experience. This basic résumé/CV worksheets will provide you with ideas you can use in your own career search.

Name: _____

Address, zip code _____

Telephone (area code): _____

E-mail address: _____

If you have a temporary address, list it also. The employer must be able to contact you immediately.

<u>Education</u> - List current or past degrees and/or certifications.

_____

_____

_____

_____

_____

<u>Continuing Education</u>

_____

_____

_____

_____

_____

Specialized Training

_____

_____

_____

_____

_____

Professional Experience Include names and dates of all paid or unpaid employment.

_____

_____

_____

_____

_____

OPTIONAL HEADINGS

Accomplishments/Achievements

_____

_____

_____

_____

_____

Athletics

_____

_____

_____

_____

_____

Awards/Scholarships

_____

_____

_____

_____

_____

Campus Involvement

_____

_____

_____

_____

_____

Certifications

_____

_____

_____

_____

_____

Clinicals

_____

_____

_____

_____

_____

Community Service

_____

_____

_____

_____

_____

Computer Software/Technology/Web Design

_____

_____

_____

_____

_____

Cooperative Education

_____

_____

_____

_____

_____

Honors

_____

_____

_____

_____

_____

International Community Service

_____

_____

_____

_____

_____

International Experience

_____

_____

_____

_____

_____

Internships

_____

_____

_____

_____

_____

Languages

_____
_____
_____
_____
_____

Leadership

_____
_____
_____
_____
_____

Licensures

_____
_____
_____
_____
_____

Mentoring

_____
_____
_____
_____
_____

National Community Service

_____
_____
_____
_____
_____

Practicum's

_____
_____
_____
_____
_____

Professional Development

_____
_____
_____
_____
_____

Professional Organizations/Memberships/Affiliations

_____
_____
_____
_____
_____

Publications

_____
_____
_____
_____
_____

Research Projects

_____
_____
_____
_____
_____

Service Learning

_____
_____
_____
_____
_____

Special Interests

_____
_____
_____
_____
_____

Specialized Research

_____
_____
_____
_____
_____

Thesis

_____
_____
_____
_____
_____

Volunteering

_____
_____
_____
_____
_____

Break down all of your work experience into specific skill headings. Add additional headings as you need them.

Management/Organizational Skills

_____
_____
_____
_____
_____

Communication Skills

_____
_____
_____
_____
_____

Special Accomplishments

_____
_____
_____
_____
_____

Leadership Experience

_____
_____
_____
_____
_____

Communication/Public Relations

_____
_____
_____
_____
_____

Quick Tip

Always create a résumé/CV based on the employer's point of view. Ask yourself this question: If you were the employer, would you be impressed by your résumé/CV? Be able to answer the question, "Why should I hire you?"

CHAPTER 7
RÉSUMÉ/CV REFERENCE GUIDE

The Résumé/CV Reference Guide visually demonstrates a formatting process that you can adapt to your own career history and skill set. This reference guide contains a master list of required résumé/CV information and optional headings. It is not a sample résumé or CV. You can review the entire guide and select any heading you feel is relevant. It is a detailed description of what can go into your résumé/CV. Never use someone else's résumé as an exact template of your own.

As a graduate, you will benefit from this step-by-step guide, complete with helpful graphics to make concepts clear, when deciding whether to prepare a Chronological, Functional, or Targeted résumé/CV, or a combination document.

The definition codes apply to the following reference guide, which has been designed for you to review after you have selected your major headings and subcategories. It is a sample of the variety of categories available for you to refer back to as needed.

14 Bold font	14B	
12 Regular font	12F	
Single line break	SL	
Double line break	DL	
Optional Heading	OH	*Optional Categories: Select one from your résumé outline.*

Full Name
Address, City, State, Zip Code
Telephone/Cell number, e-mail address (professional)

Select one or two of the optional headings to begin your résumé/CV

Optional Heading		**Objective**: *use when you are applying for a specific position.*
Optional Heading	14B	**Résumé Summary**: *use to highlight work-related experience and education.*
Optional Heading	14B	**Profile**: *It must **wow** an employer and include evidence of past experience and skills related to the position you are applying for.*
Optional Heading	14B	**Philosophy Statement**: *Use to present your personal statement of ethics regarding your career choice.*
Optional Heading	14B	**Qualifications Brief**: *Use to highlight soft skills, such as leadership abilities, problem solving, and team-building skills, especially when changing careers or job targets within your field of interest.*
DL between categories	DL	
Required Category	14B	**Education**
	DL	
	SL 12F	*Degree, major, minor, college or university, city, state, year graduated, include CPA if 3.0 or higher.* **Place category here if you are a current student or a recent graduate. If not, include education toward the end of your résumé, especially if you graduated two or more years ago.**
	DL	
Optional Heading	14B	**Thesis/Research Project**
	SL 12F	If you are a recent undergraduate or graduate student, list the name of your thesis or research project in italics. Additional text is in regular font.
	DL	
Optional Heading	14B	**Honors/Scholarships**
	SL 12F	**Use if you are a recent graduate; if not, include toward the end of your résumé. Tab over one to begin your descriptive sentences. Always use action verbs.**

	12F	NAME Page #
		If your résumé is more than one page, include your name and page number as a header on each consecutive page
	DL	
Optional Heading	14B	**Languages**
	SL 12F	**List only if you are fluent or conversational in a second language.**
	DL	
Optional Heading	14B	**Professional Experience**
	DL	
	SL 12F	Job title, name of employer, location, dates – list left or right (your preference).
	SL	
Single space within category.	SL 12F	Use descriptive statements here.
	DL	
	14B	**Leadership Experience** *paid or unpaid* Descriptive statements highlight your past job or position responsibilities.
	DL	
	SL 12F	*Title, name of employer, location, dates – list left or right (your preference).* Be specific rather than general.
	SL	
	SL 12F	**Use descriptive statements here.**
	DL	
Optional Heading	14B	**Community Service/Volunteerism** Unpaid experience is as valuable as paid, and this section can be used f it applies to your career field.
	DL	
	SL 12F	Volunteer title, employer, location, date or number of hours
	SL	
	SL 12F	Use descriptive statements here.
	DL	

	12F	NAME	Page #
Optional Heading	14B	**Internships/Cooperative Education/** **Service Learning**	
	DL		
	SL 12F	*Title, name of employer, location, dates – list left or right (your preference).*	
	SL		
	SL 12F	*Use descriptive statements here.*	
	DL		
Optional Heading	14B	**International Experience**	
	DL		
	SL 12F	**Title, employer, city, country, dates**	
	SL 12F	*Use descriptive statements here.*	
	DL		
Optional Heading	14B	**International/ National Community Service** Use these optional headings to demonstrate your global perspective.	
	DL		
	SL 12F	**Title, organization, city, state or country, dates**	
	SL		
	SL 12F	**Use descriptive statements here.**	
	DL		
Optional Heading	14B	**Professional Development**	
	DL		
	SL 12F	Workshops, seminars, in-service presentations, conferences, specialized training programs.	
	SL		
	SL 12F	Use descriptive statements here.	
	DL		
Optional Heading	14B	**Professional Affiliations/Memberships**	
	DL		

	12F	NAME Page #
	SL 12F	List complete name of your professional affiliations/ memberships and dates.
	DL	
Optional Heading	14B	**Campus Involvement**
	DL	
	SL 12F	List the name of the club or activity and the year(s) you participated. Use if you are a recent graduate or if it demonstrates your leadership skills.
	SL	
	SL 12F	**Use descriptive statements here.**
	DL	
Optional Heading	14B	**Computer Technology/Skills**
	DL	
	SL 12F	List programs (e.g., Microsoft Word, Microsoft Excel, Microsoft PowerPoint, Photoshop)
	DL	
Optional Heading	14B	**Research/Publications**
	DL	
	SL 12F	**Title of research or article, publisher, city, state, year**
	DL	
	14B	**Special Interests** **Avoid controversial topics. Use your special interests as potential ice breakers during your interviews.**
	DL	
	SL 12F	**List interests on single line, separated by a comma.**
	DL	
	14B	**Accomplishments/Achievements/Awards** **List relevant experiences you are proud of. It will give an employer additional insights into the type of individual you are.**
	DL	
	SL 12F	List accomplishments/achievements/awards, dates.

	12F	NAME	Page #
	DL		
Optional Heading	14B	**Athletics**	
	DL		
	SL 12F	List type of sport or athletic team, name of team, dates.	
	DL		
Optional Heading	14B	**References Available Upon Request**	

Quick Tip

References are not listed on your résumé, but you must be prepared to offer them on separate page.

Sample Résumé/CV Templates

As an experienced career counselor, I have learned how important it is for graduates to prepare an individualized résumé/CV. I like to say that "everyone who has written a résumé is an expert." By this I mean résumés and CVs are constantly shared with others, and sometimes they appear to be a carbon copy of someone else's. Graduates need to sort through available job search and résumé information before deciding on their format and content.

Searching for a position can be overwhelming, because graduates are faced with several choices. It's the last phase of your academic achievement. You must know why you are a great candidate when preparing an excellent résumé or CV.

Rather than give a sample résumé or CV, I have provided you with a basic résumé/CV and international résumé template.

Use the templates with the reference guide to prepare an outstanding document that will impress an employer. Another benefit to graduates of preparing your résumé/CV the hard way is knowing what you have to offer an employer, because it will be based on your employer research, networking, and information interviews. The entire process will build yourself confidence.

The International Résumé Template has been created for both international students who earn their degree in the United States, and American students who want to work globally.

Basic Résumé/CV and International Templates

Quick Tip

Include .75″ or 1″ margins on all sides. Use a simple font style. Use spell check! Do not staple résumé pages together. Use high-quality résumé paper

BASIC RÉSUMÉ TEMPLATE
FULL NAME
Address, City, State, Zip
Home Phone – Cell Phone – E-Mail

Objective/Profile/Philosophy (select one, optional heading)

Text… (12 Point)

Education (Be consistent. Names of degrees, states, and dates should be either spelled out or abbreviated throughout the résumé.)

Name of Degree, College/University, City, State, Month, Year. GPA (if 3.0 or higher)

Name of Additional Degrees, College/University, City, State, Year. GPA (if 3.0 or higher)

Honors/Scholarships (if applicable)

Name of Scholarship, Year. List most recent first.

Languages (Use this heading only if you are fluent/conversational)

Name of Language/Languages

Professional/Related Experience Internships/Practicums

Use all optional headings that apply to your career history.

Position Title, Name of Employer, City, State, Dates
- Use action verbs to describe your responsibilities in order of priority.
-
-

<u>Position Title</u>, Name of Employer, City, State, Dates
- Detailed description
-
-

<u>Position Title</u>, Name of Employer, City, State, Dates
- Detailed description
-
-

Additional Experience

<u>Position Title</u>, Name of Employer, City, State, Dates
- Use action verbs to describe your responsibilities in priority order.
-
-

Quick Tip

List additional work-related experience if it demonstrates your skills in your career or related field.

Optional Headings for All Majors (if applicable):

Quick Tip

Review and prioritize each optional heading selection.

Accomplishments/Achievements
Athletics/Athletic Leadership
Awards/Scholarships
Campus Involvement – list name of club, year(s)
Certifications – include all relevant certifications, must be current
Clinicals
Computer Software/Technology/Web Design – list of software programs
Community Service – paid or unpaid
Cooperative Education
Honors
International Community Service
International Experience
Internships

Languages
Leadership – paid or unpaid (e.g., tutor, counselor, teacher)
Licensures
Mentoring
National Community Service
Practicum
Professional Development (e.g., workshops, seminars, in-service presentations)
Professional Organizations/Memberships/Affiliations – list membership, include year(s)
Publications
Research Projects
Service Learning
Special Interests
Specialized Research
Study Abroad
Thesis
Volunteerism

CURRICULUM VITAE TEMPLATE
FULL NAME
Address, City, State, Zip
Home Phone – Cell Phone – E-Mail

Objective/Profile/Philosophy (select one, optional heading)

Quick Tip ───────────────────────────────

Your CV can be as extensive as necessary to highlight your academic qualifications, work experience, and transferable skills, including accomplishments/achievements.

Text... (12 Point)

Education (Be consistent. Names of degrees, states, and dates should be either spelled out or abbreviated throughout the résumé.)

Name of Doctoral Degree, University, City, State, Month, Year
Dissertation, *Title*, (12 Point Bold) (if applicable)

Name of Additional Degrees, College/University, City, State, Year. GPA (if 3.0 or higher)
Thesis, *Title*, (12 Point Bold) (if applicable)

Honors/Scholarships (if applicable)

Name of Scholarship/Scholarships, Year. List most recent first.

Languages (if applicable to the position)

Name of Language/Languages (Fluent/Conversational)

Professional/ Related/ Practicum/Internships Experience

Select all optional headings that apply to your career goals.

Position Title, Name of Employer, City, State, Dates
- Use action verbs to describe your responsibilities.
-
-

<u>Position Title</u>, Name of Employer, City, State, Dates
- Detailed description
-
-

<u>Position Title</u>, Name of Employer, City, State, Dates
- Detailed description
-
-

Quick Tip ———————————————————

Sub-categorize all internships, practicum's, or clinical experience before you begin this section. Combine in the same section if you have completed more than one in the same area. Lead with your career related experience first. Make every word count. Use action verbs to describe your expertise.

Additional Experience

<u>Position Title</u>, Name of Employer, City, State, Dates
- Detailed description
-
-

Optional Headings for All Majors (if applicable):

Quick Tip ———————————————————

Review and prioritize each optional heading selection. You can use several optional headings that demonstrate all of your skills and experience, including specialized achievements and accomplishments.

Accomplishments/Achievements
Athletics/Athletic Leadership
Awards/Scholarships
Campus Involvement – list name of club, year(s)
Certifications – include all relevant certifications, must be current
Clinicals
Computer Software/Technology/Web Design – list of software programs
Community Service – paid or unpaid
Cooperative Education
Honors
International Community Service

International Experience
Internships
Languages
Leadership – paid or unpaid (e.g., tutor, counselor, teacher)
Licensures
Mentoring
National Community Service
Practicum
Professional Development (e.g., workshops, seminars, in-service presentations)
Professional Organizations/Memberships/Affiliations – list membership, include year(s)
Publications
Research Projects
Service Learning
Special Interests
Specialized Research
Study Abroad
Thesis
Volunteerism

INTERNATIONAL RÉSUMÉ TEMPLATE
FULL NAME (14B)
Address, City, State, Zip (12F)
Home Phone – Cell Phone – E-Mail

Objective/Profile/Philosophy (select one) (14 Point Bold)

Text… (12 Point)

Education Be consistent. Names of degrees, states, and dates should be either spelled out or abbreviated throughout the résumé. Lead with your most recent degree.

Name of Degree, College/University, City, State, Month, Year. GPA (if 3.0 or higher, list degree and minor, if applicable).

Name of Additional Degrees, Major, College/University, City, State, Graduation Year. GPA (if 3.0 or higher).

Thesis or Research Project (12B) if applicable, *Title*

Honors/Scholarships (if applicable)

Name of Scholarship/Scholarships, Year. Lead with the most recent.
Languages (if applicable to the position, for international positions you must be fluent in your multiple languages.)

Name of Language (Fluent/Conversational)

Use the language category only if you are fluent in reading, writing, and speaking, or if you can speak conversationally.

Quick Tip

Being fluent in more than one language is important when applying for international positions.

International Internships (optional heading)

Quick Tip

Be specific and give examples of specialized skills/experience. Focus on leadership experience. Make every word count. Use action verbs to describe your transferable skills. Show rather than tell how good you are.

<u>Intern</u>, Employer, City, Country, Dates
- Detailed description in priority order
-
-

International/Professional Experience (Optional Heading)

Title, Name of Employer, City, Country, Dates
- Detailed description in priority order, using action verbs to describe your responsibilities
-
-

Title, Name of Employer, City, Country, Dates
- Detailed description in priority order
-
-

Quick Tip

Consolidate your entire work experience with a focus toward your career-related goals. Review Transferable Skills section in handbook.

International Community Service

Volunteer Title, Employer, City, Country, Dates
- Detailed description
-
-

Related Experience (paid or unpaid)
- Detailed description
-
-

Quick Tip ——————————————————————————

List additional work-related experience if it demonstrates your skills and transferable skills.

Additional Experience

- Detailed description
-
-

Quick Tip ——————————————————————————

Review and prioritize each optional heading selection.

Optional Headings for All Majors (if applicable):

Accomplishments/Achievements
Athletics/Athletic Leadership
Awards/Scholarships
Campus Involvement – list name of club, year(s)
Certifications – include all relevant certifications, must be current
Clinicals
Computer Software/Technology/Web Design – list of software programs
Community Service – paid or unpaid
Cooperative Education
Honors
International Community Service
International Experience
Internships
Languages
Leadership – paid or unpaid (e.g., tutor, counselor, teacher)
Licensures
Mentoring
National Community Service
Practicum
Professional Development (e.g., workshops, seminars, in-service presentations)
Professional Organizations/Memberships/Affiliations – list membership, include year(s)
Publications
Research Projects
Service Learning
Special Interests
Specialized Research
Study Abroad

Thesis
Volunteerism

Quick Tip ——————————————————————————

As an International graduate, you must incorporate all your relevant internships and professional experience. Demonstrate your ability and global perspective.

Advice for International/Global Candidates

An international/global candidate is a graduate who has received his or her degree in the United States. He or she may want to return to their home country to work, work in the United States, or work in another country. A global candidate is a graduate from the United States who may want to work for a US international employer or get hired in another country. The international résumé template can be adjusted to suit both categories of graduates.

1. Review your current and prior international experience to see how it relates to your current goals and objectives. If you are an international student, your résumé is usually totally different from a US version. Reevaluate your job descriptions and identify specific examples of your skills and the transferable skills all employers seek, and incorporate them into your résumé format.

2. List examples of your achievements and accomplishments, especially your communication skills, including your ability to be a team player and decision maker. You must be flexible and knowledgeable about the country you want to work in. You can do this by researching each international employers' mission and vision statements, goals, objectives, including future trends.

3. Be as detailed as possible, including no fluff or untruths. Show rather than tell how good you are with your words and descriptions.

4. Focus on using career-specific action verbs to describe your work experience in your native country; include internships, practicums, and community service.

5. Select five to ten international employers who are doing well. Focus on leaders in your field of interest. Learn what their mission and vision statements, goals, and objectives are by including the relevant transferable skills they value.

6. Talk to professionals in your career sector and ask for advice and information regarding their professional experience. Always avoid asking for a job.

7. Make sure you have one or more individuals check your résumé for errors or typos — even one can prevent you from getting an interview.

8. Make sure you meet all the travel requirements of the country in which you are applying for a position. Learn about their culture and interviewing etiquette. This will demonstrate your respect and professionalism.

9. Contact alumni who work internationally, because they will be willing to help you make contacts and offer important tips and networking opportunities.

10. Seek support and assistance from your college/university career center. Schedule an appointment for help with the entire international job search.

11. Find a career mentor who will encourage and motivate you to never give up searching for realistic career opportunities.

Résumé/CV Action Verbs for All Majors

Action verbs are important to use when preparing your résumé/CV. You want to make sure you don't repeat the same action verb at the beginning of each sentence. If you do, this limits the impact of how you describe your experience, skills, and transferable skills. You can use a thesaurus to look for words that have similar meanings. The list below is you a sampling of action verbs you can use to begin your descriptive sentences.

When analyzing your work history, take time to ask yourself, "What did I accomplish?" List your achievements on a sheet of paper and then group your statements in priority order, always focusing on the qualifications and experience needed for your potential job.

Your choice of action verbs speaks volumes about your skills and experience. Choose them wisely and increase your interview opportunities.

Sample Action Verbs

Accelerated, accepted, accomplished, accumulated, achieved, acquired, acted, activated, adapted, addressed, adjusted, administered, advanced, advertised, advised, advocated, aided, allocated, analyzed, answered, applied, appointed, appraised, approved, arbitrated, arranged, assembled, assessed, assigned, assisted, attained, augmented, authorized, awarded

Balanced, budgeted, began, boosted, briefed, built

Calculated, captured, cared, cataloged/catalogued, centralized, chaired, challenged, championed, charted, checked, clarified, classified, coached, coded, collaborated, collected, combined,, committed, communicated, compared, compiled, completed, composed, computed, computerized, conceived, conceptualized, condensed, conducted, conferred, conserved, consolidated, constructed, consulted, contacted, continued, contributed, controlled, convened, converted, conveyed, convinced, cooperated, coordinated, corrected, corresponded, counseled, crafted, created, critiqued, cultivated, customized

Debated, debugged, decided, decreased, dedicated, defined, delegated, delivered, demonstrated, designated, designed, detected, determined, developed, devised, diagnosed, directed, discovered, dispensed, dispersed, displayed, dissected, distributed, diversified, diverted, documented, drafted, drew

Earned, edited, educated, effected, elected, elicited, eliminated, emphasized, employed, enabled, enacted, encouraged, enforced, engaged, engineered, enhanced, enlarged, enlisted, ensured, established, estimated, evaluated, examined, excelled, executed, exhibited, expanded, expedited, experimented, explained, explored, expressed, extended, extracted

Fabricated, facilitated, familiarized, fashioned, filed, finalized, financed, fixed, focused, formed, formulated, fortified, fostered, found, fulfilled, furnished, furthered

Gained, gathered, generated, governed, grossed, guided

Halted, handled, hastened, headed, heightened, held, helped, hired, honed, hosted, hyperlinked, hypothesized

Identified, illustrated, implemented, improved, improvised, included, incorporated, increased, indexed, initiated, innovated, inspected, inspired, installed, instilled, instituted, instructed, insured, interacted, interpreted, intervened, interviewed, introduced, invented, inventoried, investigated, involved, issued

Joined, judged, justified, juxtaposed

Kept, keyed

Launched, learned, lectured, led, lessened, leveraged, lifted, lightened, linked, lined-up, liquidated, listed, listened, litigated, lobbied, located, logged, lowered

Maintained, managed, manipulated, manufactured, mapped, marketed, masterminded, maximized, measured, mediated, mentored, merged, mobilized, modeled, moderated, modified, monitored, motivated, multitasked

Narrowed, navigated, negotiated, netted, networked, neutralized, normalized, notarized, numbered

Observed, obtained, opened, operated, orchestrated, ordered, organized, originated, outlined, outsourced, overcame, overhauled, oversaw

Participated, perceived, performed, persuaded, photographed, piloted, pinpointed, pioneered, placed, planned, played, predicted, prepared, prescribed, presented, presided, prevented, printed, prioritized, processed, procured, produced, programmed, projected, promoted, proofread, propelled, proposed, protected, proved, provided, publicized, purchased

Qualified, questioned

Raised, ran, rated, reached, realigned, realized, reasoned, received, recognized, recommended, reconciled, recorded, recruited, rectified, recycled, reduced, referred, regained, registered, regulated, rehabilitated, related, reinforced, remodeled, rendered, renegotiated, reorganized, repaired, replaced, reported, repositioned, represented, researched, reserved, reshaped, resolved, responded, restored, restructured, retrieved, reviewed, revised, revitalized, routed

Satisfied, saved, scheduled, screened, searched, secured, selected, separated, served, shaped, shared, simplified, simulated, singled, sketched, sold, solicited, solved, sorted, spearheaded, specialized, specified, spoke, sponsored, staffed, standardized, started, stimulated, streamlined, structured, studied, submitted, suggested, summarized, supervised, supplied, supported, surpassed, surveyed, sustained, synchronized, synthesized, systematized

Tabulated, targeted, taught, terminated, tested, tightened, totaled, tracked, traded, trained, transcribed, transferred, transformed, transitioned, translated, transmitted, traveled, troubleshoot, tutored

Uncovered, understood, undertook, unified, united, updated, upgraded, used, utilized

Validated, verbalized, verified, vetted, visualized, vitalized, volunteered, voted

Weighed, welcomed, widened, won, worked, wrote

X-rayed

Yielded

Zeroed

CHAPTER 8

GETTING RESULTS FROM YOUR PORTFOLIO

In addition to your cover letter and résumé, you have the option of adding a *portfolio*. Your portfolio will contain highlights, both visual and written, of your unique background. The portfolio provides a snapshot of concrete examples of your education, work history, and creativity, including career-related objectives. For example, if you are a teacher, your portfolio may contain copies of lesson plans, student teaching evaluations, pictures of classroom activities and work centers such as biology or science. It is a results-oriented snapshot of all your career-related accomplishments.

If you are a physical or occupational therapist, you may want to include a sample outline of your in-service presentations to the health-care team or give an example of a particular treatment plan or research project. If you are a nurse or physician assistant, you may want to focus on a health education program you developed and promoted on campus or in the community. You may also want to include special certifications you have received.

Business or information technology majors might want to include a special website they have designed, listing its content, or a sample PowerPoint presentation prepared for a club or organization. If you are a liberal arts major, you might have a collection of short stories or a poetry collection. This would be important to include if you want to be an editor or work in the publishing industry. Any experience working on a student newspaper would also be relevant. You can show rather than tell the employer proof of your talents. All majors can include their experience working on grants, by providing a brief overview of the role you played in receiving a competitive grant.

Your CV portfolio can highlight specific leadership projects or research studies related to your career field. You can include community service projects and special courses you have taught. Only you can decide what to include in your portfolio. It is important to prioritize all your headings in your table of contents. Make sure it is organized and easy to read in a binder or folder.

You can bring a brief sample of your master portfolio to an interview, and when the employer invites you to ask questions, you can ask if you can share a sample of your portfolio with the interviewer or interviewing committee. The smaller version of your portfolio contains high-priority items in a folder, with no more than six or seven pages. Make several copies you can leave behind for the employer or committee to review.

Quick Tip

Portfolios document your life experience in a specific career field and are an important component of your career planning and job search process. They are a powerful self-evaluation tool. They also help you to keep track of your career progress. You can always refer back to your portfolio When you navigate toward new positions inside and outside your career field. The portfolio can help you stay focused on your professional objectives.

Your Portfolio: Ten Reminders

1. Use a detailed table of contents and subheadings. Review the optional headings in this chapter. They include education, technology, education, health, medical, liberal arts, and a basic outline for CVs in all majors. The outlines provide only a sample of headings you can use. You may add additional headings that are relevant and demonstrate your unique background.
2. Prioritize the order of your table of contents. Set your standards high and focus on your transferable skills and any experience that may be relevant to an employer.
3. Tab each section in alphabetical order and be creative with your headings.
4. Type page headings and use tabs to separate the individual sections, making sure they are easy to read.
5. Use quality bond paper for your binder or specially designed portfolio folder.
6. Protect your content with plastic insert pages.
7. Organize your portfolio from an employer's perspective. Include high-priority accomplishments first and present your entire portfolio in a visually appealing format.
8. Use bulleted statements to draw the reader to important entries.
9. Prepare a mini-portfolio (a sample of what's contained in your master portfolio) and make several copies that you can leave with an employer after an interview.
10. Mini-portfolios are ideal for employment fairs, interviewing committees, and interviews.

Portfolio Format Outlines

Below are some suggestions to help you prepare your portfolio.

Sample Portfolio: Business/Technology

Table of Contents
Achievements

Advocacy
Business Philosophy
Business Experience
Campus Involvement
Certificates
Certifications
Community Service
Computer Software
Cooperative Education
Copies of Transcripts
International Experience
Information Technology
Internships
Languages
Leadership
Licenses
National or International Service
Mentoring
Professional Associations/Affiliations
Professional Development (workshop or in-service training)
Professional Experience (paid or unpaid)
Profile
References: professional and/or character
Research Project
Résumé
Sample Activities/Presentations
Service Learning
Study Abroad Experience
Specialized Training
Supervisory Experience
Thesis Overview
Technology Skills/Programs/Languages/Web Development
Volunteerism
Work-Related Summary

Quick Tip

Your portfolio must be individualized to highlight your professional growth and development in your field. You can add additional headings continuously.

Sample Portfolio: Education

Quick Tip —————————————————————————————

This portfolio outline can be used for a variety of education positions in all employment sectors.

Table of Contents
Achievements
Advocacy
Certificates
Certifications
Community Service
Computer Software
Cooperative Education
Employer Feedback Evaluations
International Experience
Internships
Languages
Leadership Opportunities (paid or unpaid)
Masters Project
Mentoring
National/International Community Service
Professional and Academic Associations/Affiliations
Professional Development (workshops, in-service training)
Profile for your particular educational field
References: professional and/or character
Résumé
Sample Activities (unit plans, computer technology in the classroom)
Service Learning
Special Classroom Projects (e.g., learning center examples)
Special Interests
Student Teaching Evaluations
Student/Parent Feedback (letters, thank-you notes, pictures)
Study Abroad
Supervising Teacher Evaluations
Supervisory Experience
Teaching Experience (lesson plans/homework)
Teaching Philosophy
Technology Skills/Experience
Thesis Overview
Training Experience (describe experience related to the position you are applying for)
Training Presentations/Workshops, In-Service Presentations
Volunteerism

Quick Tip

Teachers and educators have transferable skills to apply for nonteaching positions. Make sure to highlight your leadership, organizational, and leadership experience.

Sample Portfolio: Health/Medical

Quick Tip

Prepare a portfolio that highlights your experience in the field of health/medicine. Be creative. All headings are optional, and you can include additional headings in the medical field.

Table of Contents
Achievements
Additional Graduate Coursework
Advanced Clinical Assessments
Advocacy
Campus Involvement
Case Studies
Certificates
Certifications
Clinical Evaluation Summaries
Committee Involvement
Community Service
Computer Software
In-service Presentations/Sample
International Experience
Languages
Leadership
Leadership Experience (paid or unpaid)
Medical Experience
Medical-Related Experience
Mentoring
National/International Community Experience
Patient Care Philosophy
Patient/Client Thank-You notes (optional)
Practicum
Professional Development
Professional and Academic Associations/Affiliations
Profile
References: professional and/or character
Research Project
Research Publications

Résumé
Rotation Highlights
Sample Client/Patient Achievements
Sample Treatment Plans
Special Interests
Specialized Area of Interest
Study Abroad
Technology
Thesis Overview
Volunteerism
Work-Related Experience/Skills

Quick Tip

Review your life experience and include all relevant transferable skills. Design your portfolio to highlight your strong work ethic and leadership skills.

Sample Portfolio: Liberal Arts

Quick Tip

The liberal arts portfolio can be used for all fields. Create your table of contents based on your unique transferable skills and special interests. Your portfolio can be used for all employment sectors.

Table of Contents
Accomplishments
Achievements
Additional Experience
Advocacy
Campus Involvement
Certificates
Certifications
Collaboration Opportunities
Committee Involvement
Community Service
Computer Software
Cooperative Education
Grant Writing Experience
Innovative Activities
International Experience
Internship Evaluations (or feedback from supervisors)
Internships

Languages
Leadership
Licenses
Mentoring
National/International Community Service
Overview of Professional Experience
Philosophy/Profile (occupation specific)
Professional Development (workshops, in-service training)
Professional and Academic Associations/Affiliations
Projects
Publications
References: professional and/or character
Related Experience
Research
Research Project
Résumé
Sample Activities
Service Learning
Special Interests
Specialized Training
Study Abroad
Technology Skills/Programs/Languages/Web Development
Thesis Overview
Transcripts (copies)
Volunteer Projects
Work-Related Experience

Sample Portfolio: Curriculum Vitae

Quick Tip

CV Portfolios can be extensive and have no limitations to the number of pages or headings. The contents of the portfolio depend on your education, research skills, and work experience.

Table of Contents
Accomplishments/Achievements
Additional Graduate Coursework
Advocacy
Clinical Experience
Community Service
Cooperative Education
Curriculum Vitae
Fellowships

Grants
International Experience
Laboratory Experience
Leadership
Licensures/Certificates/Certifications
Mentoring
National/International Community Service
Philosophy Statement or Profile
Presentations/Seminars/Workshops
Professional and Academic Associations/Affiliations
Professional/Career/Vocational/Research Objective(s)
Publications/Works in Progress
References: professional and/or character
Research
Research Projects
Service Learning
Specialized Professional Experience
Study Abroad
Teaching/Training Experience
Technology Skills/Web Development
Thesis/Dissertation Abstract
Volunteerism

CHAPTER 9
WRITING A WINNING COVER LETTER

Your résumé is finished and you're ready to actually apply for positions. But have you prepared a winning cover letter, or are you feeling frustrated by the entire process? It's understandable if you are confused, because a good cover letter requires time, research, and knowledge of an employer's list of qualifications. If you take the time to write a master cover letter, you will be able to use its basic content to apply for many positions.

The only changes you will have to make to your cover letter when applying for various positions pertain to your employer research. Your qualifications and experience can be easily adapted to each position you are applying for. This chapter takes you step by step through the process of writing a great cover letter. Graduates are usually so busy they think they can draft a cover letter quickly and it will work. Well, sometimes it does — for example, if the employer is desperate for specific qualifications that you possess. However, most employers value a good cover letter. As I've said throughout this handbook, there are exceptions to every rule.

If you want to ensure positive results, make your cover letter a priority. If you are concerned about your spelling or typos, always have a couple of individuals edit and proofread your cover letter. The staff at your career services center is always available to help you. You can and will write a winning cover letter if you try your best.

Cover Letter Quiz

What is the purpose of your cover letter?

Select number 1, 2, 3, or 4

1. To get you an interview.   _____
2. Just a formality and no big deal.   _____

3. It's a fun thing to do.
4. It serves as an introduction to your résumé.   _____

    The answer is #4. The cover letter serves as a self-introduction to the employer, but it's the résumé that generates interviews. Having said that, attaching a winning cover letter is important. It can impress an employer or leave her shaking her head with disbelief. Employers can always tell if you did your homework on the position posted by their organization.

    Your cover letter is like a TV advertisement. When you see a commercial, you have an instant reaction. You either keep watching it and want to try the product, ignore it, or change the channel. The analogy is clear. Your cover letter gets the same response as a commercial. The employer will like it or they won't. In reality, they want to like your cover letter, because it makes their job easier. Often your cover and résumé are prescreened by someone in their personnel department. If it generates interest it gets passed on directly to the employer or hiring committee chair. If not, it gets put into the NO pile. If you think of your cover letter as the entry point into your career field, you will do the work and be proud of yourself.

Cover Letters Facts

- The cover letter is the finishing touch to your job search presentation. It complements your résumé and is an important aspect of your employment search.
- Cover letters are helpful because they reach the employer before you do. They have the power to open closed doors.
- Your cover letter must contain relevant information, with action verbs that come alive on the page. It is targeted to a specific position opening and entices an employer to review your résumé. Generic cover letters often get rejected.
- A generic can be spotted within several seconds. They take little time to write and are usually sent to many employers simultaneously. The content is questionable and its impact is minimal.
- The most important component of a winning cover letter is its accuracy. Research each potential employer's mission, vision, goals, and objectives. Your research is demonstrated in the body of your cover letter and proves to an employer why you are the perfect match for the position.
- The reason for writing a winning cover letter is to rise to the top of the list of job candidates. Write the best cover letter you can to convince an employer to review your résumé and call you in for an interview.

Cover Letters Misconceptions

1. Cover letters are unnecessary because employers only want to see a résumé.
2. Its okay to send the same cover letter to all employers.
3. Cover letters are easy to prepare.
4. You don't have to do any research to write a good cover letter.
5. Stretching the truth is acceptable.

6.   Typos are overlooked by the reader.
7.   Only some people need to write a cover letter.
8.   I've never written one in the past, so I don't need to write one now.
9.   I'll just copy one and change a few details and no one will know the difference.
10.   Cover letters just don't work. I just sent out a hundred and never got an interview.

Quick Tip

Make sure you know exactly what the position opening requires. Never wing it. The employer will list the qualifications in priority order. Be prepared to identify your transferable skills related to the position. Give specific examples using their key words.

How to Analyze Job Requirements

You can analyze job requirements by researching the employer's company/organizational profile, as well as their vision or mission statements. Read brochures describing their services and recruitment methods. Gain as much knowledge as you can by researching the employer's website. Research company/organizational problems, issues, concerns, and management styles. Read and study the job description. This information is the framework of your cover letter. Use it to identify the type of candidate the employer wants to hire.

In your cover letter you can refer to your résumé and give additional examples demonstrating your job-specific abilities, talents, and transferable skills. Approach this process from an employer's point of view. Convince the reader you have most, if not all, of the position requirements. Use your occupational research to prioritize your statements. Most employers list the desired job skills according to the responsibilities of each position open. Study the job posting and list of job qualifications, and tailor your cover letter to each position opening.

Study the job description line by line. The qualifications will be listed in priority order. Review the ad several times. Be sure you understand what the employer is looking for in terms of experience, education, skills, and transferable skills. Try to talk with someone who has the same title or similar work experience. Apply for the position even if you are missing some of the qualifications. The experience you do have may compensate for some requirement you don't have. By studying the job description carefully you will feel confident and well qualified.

Believe it or not, it can take several hours to prepare a master cover letter. Once completed, you can use it as a foundation for all additional cover letters. Each cover letter must be focused on the employer's needs. The key component to your cover letter is your employer research. The payoff will come when your résumé is reviewed and an interview is scheduled. Please take time to prepare a quality promotional piece about yourself. Its contents will grab the employer's interest and insure your résumé will be read. Most employers receive many boring cover letters, so try to make yours stand out.

Quick Tip

Make sure your cover letter stands out among the crowd. Your cover letter must be on the same quality paper as your résumé. Have it proofread by others. Double check its content and make sure it's a perfect reflection of you as a candidate.

Your cover letter may be read and screened by a human resource manager, recruiter, search committee, or the person who will work with the new employee. It may be passed on from person to person, until it reaches the top of the hiring chain. Your cover letter will open doors, and your résumé will generate interviews.

List below are detailed examples of how to analyze the job requirements listed in the position description. This is only a sample of the most asked-for qualifications.

1.   **Degree**

If the ad doesn't specify what type of degree is required, you will have flexibility. If it requires a specific degree, you will have to mention in your cover letter how your education can benefit the employer.

2.   **Communication Skills**

Provide concrete examples of how you have used your verbal, nonverbal, and written communication skills. What did you accomplish when you used them? How can they be transferred to the job opening?

3.   **Organizational Skills**

Show how your organizational skills relate to the position requirements. You can do this if you describe your accomplishments. Refer to your résumé, but use different examples in your cover letter.

4.   **Record of Accomplishments**

How did you help your former or current employer? Describe what you are most proud of. Explain briefly in one or two sentences how you made a difference.

5.   **Leadership Skills**

Tell employers the qualities you have demonstrated in your current or previous jobs and how you were an asset to the company or organization. Include your philosophy of leadership. Briefly describe how your leadership skills will be beneficial to the employer.

Cover Letter Worksheet

Position Description

_____

_____

_____

_____

_____

List Keywords in Priority Order

_____

_____

_____

_____

_____

Describe your current or past work experience using each keyword. Give at least three examples of specific activities. Tailor your answers to the job requirements.

Keyword — Example of Activity

_____

_____

_____

_____

Keyword — Example of Activity

_____

_____

_____

_____

Keyword — Example of Activity

_____

_____

_____

_____

Keyword — Example of Activity

_____

_____

_____

_____

_____

Answer the following questions. Write "Yes" or "No" after each question.
- Have I researched the qualifications and requirements of the position opening? __
- Do I know the employer's mission or philosophy? __
- Can I describe why I am the best candidate for the job? __

If you have answered "no" to one or more questions, go back and complete your research immediately.

Summarize in five statements why you are the perfect candidate.

1. _____
2. _____
3. _____
4. _____
5. _____

Cover Letter Checklist

- **Focus** on your job target. Many graduates neglect to research a potential employer.
- **View** each cover letter as an accurate description of your qualifications for the position you are applying for.
- **Show** your qualifications. Know how you will fit into their work culture and environment.
- **Always** use quality bond paper for a professional appearance.
- **Treat** your cover letter as a five-second infomercial.
- **Make** your content substance rather than fluff.
- **Highlight** and expand on your work experiences listed in your résumé, using specific examples.
- **Target** each cover letter to a specified or potential job opening.
- **Ask** permission to include the name of the person who referred you in the cover letter (if you have been referred to the job opening). Do so in the first paragraph, "Sally Doe suggested I apply for the position opening …"
- **Use** your master cover letter to format others and print your cover letter on quality bond paper (20 or 25 lbs).

- **Promote** your résumé one cover letter at a time. Make sure you proofread for typos and have at least two readers check for errors.
- **Address** your cover letter to the decision maker, if possible.
- **Remember**, cover letters count. A résumé without a cover letter will short-circuit your job hunt. Please allow your self-confidence to be reflected within the text of your cover letter.
- **Follow up** with a telephone call to the employer within seven to ten days to make sure they received your cover letter/résumé/CV and to find out when the interview process will begin.

Cover Letter Outline for All Career Sectors

Date

Your name
Street Address
City, State, Zip

Employer's Name
Title
Company-Firm-Organization
City, State, Zip

Dear _____, [always use a name if possible. If not, use Representative, Recruiter, Director, or Manager. Avoid using Sir, Madam, or Whom It May Concern. Make sure you check the spelling and use correct salutation (e.g., Ms., Miss, Mrs.)]

First Paragraph

Apply for the position [e.g., I am applying for the position of (specific position) with (name of company or organization)]. Make a brief statement telling the employer why you would be an asset [e.g., My education and leadership experience in _____ would be beneficial to your organization].

Second Paragraph

Do your research. Paraphrase the employee's mission, vision, or goals [e.g., As my research indicates, XYZ's commitment to excellence matches my philosophy of _____]. Summarize your strengths and achievements. Show rather than tell why you are the best person for the job [e.g., My strengths include _____, _____, and _____]. Be specific and prove why you are a good candidate with your words. You can expand on the information contained in your résumé, but never repeat exactly the same words and descriptions. Here you have an opportunity to go into specifics that relate to the position opening. Study the qualifications carefully and stay focused on your unique skills. This paragraph must be prioritized on the requirements of the position. You can refer to your résumé when you expand on a specific description or experience.

Third Paragraph

Keep it brief [e.g., I look forward to an opportunity to interview for a position opening. Thank you for your consideration].

Sincerely,

[Name]

Avoid Dear Sir, Mr., or Ms. unless you are certain how the individual wants to be addressed. Each employer prefers to be referred to in a certain way. Several graduates I've worked with used the title "Ms." when the employer wanted to be called "Mrs." It doesn't happen often, and you can easily find out what an employer's preference is by looking in the company directory, by looking through an organization online, or by calling personnel and asking. Also, make sure you spell and pronounce the contact's name correctly if you are called for an interview. Your first paragraph must indicate your reason for writing. It must be clear and concise.

Your second paragraph provides an opportunity to make a good first impression on paper. It serves as a solid introduction to your value as an employee.

There is no need to tell the employer when they can call you or to include your cell/telephone number if it will be included on your résumé. It is acceptable to contact the employer within seven to ten days to inquire if the interview process has been completed or when a candidate will be selected.

Scoring Your Cover Letter

This quiz is a great way to reinforce what you have learned about writing a winning cover letter. You are a graduate who is prepared successfully to market yourself to employers. Your score will determine whether you need to review this chapter again.

No.	Question	Yes	No	Score
1.	Have you analyzed the current or potential job opening?	Yes (+1)	No (-2)	
2.	Can you define your strong points and give examples of your job-related strengths?	Yes (+3)	No (-2)	
3.	Can you *show* rather than *tell* an employer how you can provide a strong work ethic?	Yes (+3)	No (-3)	
4.	Have you ever talked to individuals who have a similar position?	Yes (+2)	No (-1)	
5.	Have you focused on the employer's mission, vision, and purpose?	Yes (+3)	No (-2)	

No.	Question	Yes	No	Score
6.	Can you back up your accomplishments with specific examples of successes?	Yes (+5)	No (-3)	
7.	Have you had your cover letter proofread by someone else?	Yes (+6)	No (-5)	
8.	Is your cover letter homework completed and documented?	Yes (+5)	No (-5)	

Scoring Results

+28 points
Excellent! Your cover letter will be successful.

+27 to +22 points
Great! An almost a perfect cover letter. Critique your cover letter again. Revisions are the key to success.

+21 to +15 points
You're getting there! Review chapter 9 and continue to improve the quality of your cover letter by defining the reasons why you're the best person for the job.

+14 to +1 points
Keep plugging away. You are off to a good start. Take the time to do your homework on yourself and the employer. It will insure that your cover letter will generate interest.

-1 to -14 points
Your cover letter needs a major revision or it will go into the circular file (wastebasket). To get back on track, review chapter 9.

-15 to -21 points
Don't give up! Continue to review and revise.

-23 points
Start again. Research, revise, and rethink the entire cover letter process. Ask yourself if you really want the position you are applying for. Are you playing it safe and applying for a job you really don't want? It's okay to change your mind. If you decide to continue on, you must commit to writing a first-class cover letter.

CHAPTER 10
INTERVIEW REALITIES

This chapter will prepare you for an actual interview in several ways. It will help you avoid the pitfalls of "winging it" in an interview. It will give you an opportunity to practice what you've learned about the process. And it will help you learn from other graduates' mistakes.

When you get offered an interview you have only one chance to get an offer or to be selected for a second or third round of interviews. Employers want to hire graduates who are qualified and have completed their company or organizational research. You must know exactly why you're the best person for the job. It is important to approach the interview process form an employer's perspective. What type employee would *you* want to hire?

If you are prepared, you will have the confidence to convince the decision maker you are the best candidate. You have to create a positive first impression. Preparing for the interview will help you to feel less stress, because you will be ready for unexpected questions. You will easily be able to answer the question, "Why *should* I *hire* you?" It's also an opportunity to demonstrate professionalism.

If you are prepared you will have the ability to impress and convince decision makers to consider you as the top candidate.

A difficult interview can be a gut-wrenching experience. It will often take you by surprise and make you feel as though you've been thrown up against a brick wall. The best way to prepare for traumatic interviews is to complete a self-assessment of how you handle interviews. All interviews are learning experiences. They are opportunities to evaluate employers and your job target goals.

When and if you experience a difficult interview, immediately begin to review the realities of the interviewing process.

Reality #1   **There are exceptions to every single rule of interviewing. Learn from the exceptions and view each interview as unique.**

You must tailor your interview style to each position opening. Be prepared to be a walking advertisement. First impressions count. You can convince an employer you are the best person for the job if you demonstrate professionalism, preparedness, and personality.

Reality #2   **Successful interviewees are seldom those who "wing it."**

The odds of getting an interview are within your control. You can make it happen! Employers want to hire the perfect employee, and you want to be hired by the perfect boss. Increase your chance of getting hired by being thoroughly prepared for the unexpected.

To avoid difficult interviews, finish your homework. Preparing for the interview is a process that begins when you set your job target, write a résumé, prepare a cover letter, and talk with others in your employment field.

Reality #3   **Unemployed job hunters need to prepare for an interview as if they were entering a horse race with a photo finish.**

You can get hired or rejected in an instant. The determining factors will be your personality, dress, enthusiasm, work and work-related experience, and self-confidence. Act like a winner and you will be perceived as one!

Reality #4   **You must make a commitment to research future employers. You must know their mission, vision, achievements, problems, concerns, and global perspectives.**

Many job hunters omit the research phase of the interview process. Reject the idea that it's a waste of time. Make it a priority for each interview. Research will prepare you to be the best candidate for the job. Employer information is readily available on websites, in professional journals and publications, and in books in print. Information from individuals already employed there can also be very useful.

All graduates need to prepare for both traditional and behavioral interviews. Both techniques may be used in the same interview. It all depends on the employer's preference. Practice interviews can help give you confidence and help you to learn exactly the type of response an employer looks for when hiring. You can practice with your friends, family, and professionals who work in your career field, including career counselors who work in your college or university career service centers.

The interviewer's role is to assess each candidate's skills. Their purpose is to develop questions, conduct interviews, and evaluate your work-related experience. They look for individuals who are well rounded and personable.

The interview process is one of the most important aspects of the job search. You have only one chance to make an impression so you get a job offer or are selected for a second or third round of interviews.

Traditional and Behavioral Interviews

Traditional interviews focus on your work history, skills, and transferable skills relating to the position you are applying for. Most of the questions are designed to generate a specific response with proven outcomes, based on past interviewee responses. The interviewer will assess each graduate's answers in addition to their first impressions, both verbal and nonverbal. Many interviews are a combination of both the traditional and behavioral interview.

Behavioral interviews are based on both past and current job performance, as well as how this relates to the skills required for the opening. You can expect to encounter behavioral interviews often. Employers use both types of interviews when they want to cover all their bases. The Behavioral interview goes beyond the traditional interview, applying a systemic method to determine the qualifications of each candidate. In such an interview, the employer analyzes skills that are important to a specific job. The premise of the questions is that past performance is a predictor of future job success.

The behavioral interview allows graduates to compete with experienced candidates. This creates a level playing field. You may get asked negative as well as positive, open-ended questions. For example, "Can you give me an example of a time when you were faced with an unorganized team member and a deadline to meet? How did you handle the situation? You want to be able to turn a negative situation into a positive outcome or learning experience.

You need to be prepared to give a description of a personal experience, giving specific examples and information on how you handled the situation.

In both the traditional and the behavioral interview, employers want to see if you are personable and a team player with leadership skills. They also want you to have the ability to work independently, and they want to see whether you have integrity.

My advice to all graduates is to take the interviewing process seriously. Practice both types of interviews. Use your college or university career center to schedule time for mock interviews, and attend interviewing workshops. You can generate job offers if you prepare well in advance of your interview appointment.

The sample traditional and behavioral interview questions are the most popular questions. You must be able to answer them spontaneously. I know you can do it if you try.

Sample Traditional Interview Questions

Tell me about yourself. What the employer really wants to know is how your experience and skills qualify you for the job.

Why do you want to work for us? The interviewer is trying to find out if you really know what the position requires and how you will fit in.

What are your strengths and weaknesses? How well do you know yourself? Name one of your strong points and give an example, focusing on a strength the job will require. Never say you have no weaknesses; select a weakness and indicate what you have done to improve upon it. Never select weakness that will red flag an employer (e.g., "I'm always late.").

What do you want to be doing in the next five years? Focus on professional growth and higher levels of experience.

What is your philosophy of your occupation? Be able to share your philosophy spontaneously and naturally, not verbatim from a prepared text.

Why should we hire you? Know why you are the best candidate. Give examples of how you will help the employer to meet their visions, goals, and objectives.

Sample Behavioral Interview Questions

Give me an example of a time when you seemed unable to solve a work-related problem, and how were you able to find a solution? Be prepared to tell how you handled tough problems. Identify the strategies you used. Be specific.

Tell me how you exhibited leadership skills in the past, and give specific examples of how they made a difference. Think of the qualities of a leader and describe your leadership skills. Include examples of the results of your leadership abilities.

Describe the qualities of a perfect boss and give examples of how you have promoted team building among employees. Your explanations will give the employer a bird's-eye view of the supervision or management style you prefer.

Behavioral interviewers avoid questions that are hypothetical. They want candidates to remember a *specific* experience related to the question. Usually they continue to probe for answers.

Behavioral interviews benefit the candidate by enabling you to showcase all your skills and transferable skills, including those from paid or unpaid positions, such as internships, volunteer, or community service. It is critical to practice behavioral interviewing ahead of time. Doing so will increase your odds of getting a job offer.

Pre-Interview Questions

1. Do I really want the job? Explain why.

_____
_____
_____
_____
_____

2. Have I completed all my employer homework? Explain what you have done.

_____
_____
_____
_____
_____

3. What are my specific qualifications and strengths as a candidate?

_____
_____
_____
_____
_____

Interview Myths Checklist

Sometimes you can do everything correctly and still not generate job offers. This happens for a variety of reasons. Employers often tell stories about the unusual interviewing behavior of a candidate. Often they are used to demonstrate to potential graduates what *not* to do during an interview. The "Interview Myths Checklist" will help you to decide if your interview behavior is based on myths or realities.

Write "Yes" or "No" after each statement.

- Have you ever made the following comments after an interview?
  "Rejections only happen to me." _____
  "The job was already filled before the interview." _____
  "I bet the job was given to a friend of a friend." _____
  "I'm sure the qualifications changed after the interview." _____
  "My salary expectations were too high/low." _____

"I'm too mature. They wanted a younger candidate (or vice versa)." ____

"I should have done my employer research." ____

"I was under/over qualified." ____

"The interviewer told me my references were less than enthusiastic." ____

"I must have a problem because I keep getting interviews and not the job." ____

- All interviewers are experts. ____
- Personnel recruiters make all the hiring decisions. ____
- You must dress for the job, not for the interview. ____
- A handshake has little importance to the interviewer. ____
- *Tell me about yourself* means you should give your age, marital status, etc. ____
- Always ask about salary and benefits during your first interview. ____
- It's okay to bluff and expand the truth. ____
- If the interviewer asks you if you have any questions, say no. ____
- During the interview, ask about the job responsibilities because it demonstrates your interest. ____
- Tell the interviewer how difficult your last employer was to work for. ____
- Bring a friend along for company. They can wait in the reception area. ____

If you checked yes to any of the above statements, you are not alone. Interviewing myths stem from job rejections and grow and expand from job hunter to job hunter. Myths contain threads of truth. It's up to you to sort out fact from fiction.

The fact is that interviewing is a skill. Think of the first time you learned to ride a bike or play an instrument. Was it easy? Was it challenging? Did you have to keep on practicing and trying until you were successful? How many times did you fail? Was it important to you? Were you determined to learn? Did you keep at it until you got it right?

The art of interviewing can be learned if you are motivated, if you practice, and if you expect to win a job offer. Interviewing myths create opportunities to learn the truth. Each employment sector has different interviewing guidelines. It's the job hunter's responsibility to prepare for each individual interview.

Interview Truths

Interview truths reflect the reality of the interview process. They provide factual information that can help you prepare and understand what can happen before, during, and after an interview. Interview truths are vital to all graduates, especially if you are generating interviews and no job offers, or you are having problems not getting an interview. Each truth can open your eyes to the complex world of interviewing.

1. Job rejections are a fact of life and provide opportunities to learn and focus on the next interview.

2. Sometimes the interview is a mere formality to meet the required number of candidates, even when a front-runner has already emerged.

3. Who you know *does* count! Your network of contacts opens the door to hidden job opportunities.

4. Job qualifications may change midstream depending on economic conditions.

5. Your salary expectations must be reasonable and based on accurate salary guidelines.

6. If you think you're too old or too young to get hired, you are.

7. Research is critical to matching your skills and qualifications to potential employers.

8. You can be perceived to be over/under qualified for a position, unless you change the employer's perception of your abilities.

9. Make sure individuals you ask for a reference can give you an excellent rather than a mediocre one.

10. If your interviews do not generate job offers, review your interviewing style immediately.

11. Most interviewers are not experts. It is often a role that is delegated to them by a supervisor.

12. Personnel representatives and recruiters sometimes interview, screen, and select potential candidates for the real decision makers.

13. Dress for the interview and not the job. This demonstrates professionalism and self-confidence.

14. "Tell me about yourself" is asked by the interviewer to find out how your previous work experience matches the current job requirements.

15. Salary and benefit questions should only be asked *after* you have been given a job offer, unless an employer asks you for a salary range first. If asked, you can respond by saying, "It's negotiable." Suggest a salary range based on your bottom line, or ask the interviewer to share a budget range.

16. Be prepared to ask the employer specific questions. Your research will help you to decide what to ask.

17. Never ask the employer what they do. It's a tip-off that you didn't do your homework.

18. Be careful to avoid sharing negative information about former employers. Doing so raises yellow flags. Chances are the interviewer will be afraid to hire you.

19. The interview process is not an event for friends and family. Always arrive alone.

20. All interviews count and give you valuable experience.

21. You will get a job offer if you keep generating interviews.

22. Never take job rejections personally.

23. Focus on why an employer should hire you.

24. Practice mock interviewing so you can know all the answers by heart.

25. Be prepared for telephone, in-person, Skype, or group interviews, both large and small.

26. Always arrive at least fifteen minutes early.

27. Never have alcohol prior to an interview.

28. Never bring a friend or relative, or your children, on an interview.

29. Do your research before the interview, because the employer will ask you what you know about the company.

30. Never initiate questions about vacation days, salary, or benefits before you get the job offer.

31. Avoid saying anything negative about a prior employer.

32. Know why you're the best candidate for the job.

33. Practice interviewing prior to the interview.

34. Never eat or talk on the telephone during an interview.

35. Make sure your handshake is confident, not wimpy or too strong.

36. Being late for an interview is disrespectful.

37. Do a dry run to make sure you know how to get to the interview site, where to park, and how to enter the building.

38. Always be polite to the gatekeeper, secretary, or administrative assistant. They are critical connections to the employer.

39. Send a thank-you note to the interviewer within twenty-four hours.

Quick Tip

You can and will generate job offers if you persevere and learn from each interview experience. Always ask for help and advice from professionals in and outside your field. Find an interview mentor who will evaluate your interview image.

All interviewers play a guessing game. Which candidate will be a star employee? Interviewing is a game with rules that change within each employment sector and according to the company or organizational structure and financial situation of the employer.

Successful job hunters never give up and never take "no" as a sign of failure. They keep improving their interviewing skills and realize they are but one interview away from a job offer.

Dressing for the Interview

Dressing professionally for an interview is important; because it shows an employer you are detail oriented and take pride in your appearance. Both men and women should always stick to the basics. Select conservative color combinations. Choose an outfit in which you will feel both comfortable and confident.

Advice for Women

Choose conservative suits, skirts, blouses, or pantsuits in basic color combinations such as black, navy, grey, or brown. Lighter shades are also acceptable. Dresses and skirts with coordinated jackets or blazers can be mixed and matched for versatility. Include a white or colorful basic blouse, shell, or sweater to round out your wardrobe. Power colors include a touch of red in your accessories (e.g., pin, scarf). Your fingernails should be cleaned and your nail polish conservative.

Never wear your skirt or dress too short. Jewelry should be professional and conservative. Keep your perfume light; you don't want it to reach the employer before you do. Avoid low necklines and open-toed shoes or sandals, and make sure your shoes are clean and polished. Never wear casual pants or jeans. Remove nose and eyebrow rings and tongue posts for the interview. Never chew gum during an interview. If you are a smoker, make sure your clothing is smoke free. Your makeup should fit the occasion. Cover tattoos if possible, until all generations find them acceptable. Always turn off your cell phone during an interview.

Advice for Men

Stick to the basics. Wear a suit or slacks and blazer in conservative colors such as navy, black, grey, brown, or tan. Select your shirts and ties in coordinated colors. Ties should be conservative in nature and color unless interviewing in a creative field. For example, in the field of education, teachers can wear colorful ties or ties with ABCs on them to help them stand out from the crowd. Often employers in the technology field accept nontraditional interview attire, unless there is a standardized corporate dress code. Err on the side of conservatism. Avoid wearing everyday wear or jeans. Remember, you are dressing for the interview, not the job. Your shoes should be in a basic color, such as black or brown, and should be polished. Your fingernails must be groomed and your hair cut appropriately.

You can mix and match your interview clothing for each interview. Remove nose, eyebrow rings, and tongue posts; if possible, cover visible tattoos until all generations find them acceptable.

It is important to have your interview wardrobe pressed and clean for each interview. Your cologne should be lightly scented. If you are a smoker, make sure your clothing is smoke free. Never use your cell phone during an interview, because it will give the interviewer the impression that you are not taking the interview seriously. Never chew gum during an interview.

Quick Tip

For men and women
If you have limited funds, you can find professional clothing for men and women at second-hand stores and many social service agencies. The cost of cleaning the clothes will be worth the investment. Review dressing for success books and select an outfit based on your body type and a conservative style you are comfortable in.

Your Interview Image

Is your interview image real or an illusion? If it's real, it represents a self-confident and self-assured candidate. If it's an illusion, it's staged, improvised, or make-believe, and the interviewer will have doubts about your credibility. Your interview image must reflect a qualified, self-assured candidate.

A favorable interview image begins from the inside out. Whether you're a new graduate or retiree beginning a second career, you must do your homework. This consists of an accurate self-evaluation of your skills and transferable skills. It means believing you are the best candidate, then proving it during the interview process.

Know what the employer is looking for in terms of qualifications, responsibilities, and employee characteristics. What qualities do you have that will be an asset? Your "inside" interviewing image reflects work-related attitudes, assertiveness, and enthusiasm. Being self-assured and confident is an important component of your persona.

Market yourself as an individual who will provide concrete benefits to the employer. The way you communicate, verbally and nonverbally, will make an instant first impression. **A confident handshake is expected. A weak handshake projects weakness, while an overly firm handshake suggests that the candidate is overcompensating.** The interviewer will take notice either way.

Review several interviewing books, scan the table of contents, and you will notice that interviewer expectations are universal.

Quick Tip

Remember, even when your interview image is a perfect reflection of who you are, interviewing can often be a game of chance. Decide to take job rejections as a learning experience and an opportunity to find the right employer. Choose to never give up in your search for the right position.

Telephone interviews have become an important screening device for employers. Especially in difficult economic conditions, they can save time and money. Being able to hear a candidate's voice and initial responses to questions helps an employer decide whether to actually meet the candidate. Job hunters need to prepare for a telephone interview the same way they would prepare for a traditional or behavioral interview.

The interview may be as brief as ten minutes or as long as an hour or more. You may be interviewed by one person, several individuals, or a committee. Follow-up telephone interviews are often conducted.

You must practice and prepare in advance of your scheduled interview appointment. Know why you are the best candidate for the position. Learn about the employer's mission, vision, and goals. Never wing it on the telephone. Always be prepared for a variety of traditional and behavioral interview questions. You must also be knowledgeable regarding your salary requirements.

Whether you are using a landline or cell phone, make sure your call will not be interrupted. Plan ahead and make sure your call-waiting function does not interrupt the interview process. Never put an interviewer on hold with another call unless it's an emergency. Always be professional, and be available during your scheduled interview time. Preparing for telephone interviews ahead of time can help you be a less stressed, more confident candidate.

Telephone Interview Kit

Plan ahead of your interview by putting together a small box filled with your telephone interview supplies. These should include the following:

- A pen or pencil with a few blank sheets of paper to take notes during your interview.
- A copy of your résumé or CV and the job description you are applying for.
- Information regarding your employer research, including their mission, vision, and goals.
- A calendar and Post-It notes.
- A list of responses to key interview questions, such as "Tell me about yourself," "What are your strengths and weaknesses," and "Tell me about a time you demonstrated leadership."
- Organize and label all your paperwork so you can refer to it during your interview.

Quick Tip

Select a special quiet place to conduct your telephone interview. If available, it is preferable to use a landline phone to insure a good connection.

Telephone Interview Tips

- Be professional when you answer the telephone and use a professional tone of voice.
- Make sure your call-waiting message has a brief, professional message.
- Always practice your interview skills prior to the actual telephone interview by asking a friend to tape record a mock interview.
- Take a few deep breaths and speak clearly and slowly.
- Quickly write the name and title of the interviewer or interviewers and only address them by their first name if they ask you to.

- Listen to the questions carefully and take your time before answering.
- Be prepared to answer traditional and behavioral interview questions.
- During the interview, never smoke or chew gum, and have a glass of water ready if you get thirsty.
- Always thank the interviewer at the end of the call and immediately follow up with a personalized thank-you letter.

Be Prepared to Ask Questions

Usually, toward the end of an interview you will be given the opportunity to ask questions. Always prepare your questions ahead of time. Have them written down and ready to read if you are concerned that you will forget them. You will only need three or four questions to ask the interviewer.

Ten Optional Employer Questions

1. Is this a new position or will the individual selected be replacing another professional?
2. Will there be opportunities for in-service training and mentoring?
3. Are upper-level positions usually filled from within or posted outside the organization?
4. How do you encourage innovation?
5. Do you have a high rate of employee retention?
6. Are there leadership opportunities available to all employees?
7. What are the most important qualities you look for in new employees?
8. Will the person selected have educational opportunities and additional training?
9. How are employees evaluated?
10. What is a typical day like?

Quick Tip ───────────────────────────

Prepare questions that will demonstrate you have researched the employer and understand their issues and concerns.

Handling Inappropriate Questions

Occasionally during an interview you will be asked an inappropriate question. This can be difficult and disarming. On occasion, an employer may even ask a question you feel is illegal. If this happens, you have a decision to make. You can ask the interviewer how the question is relevant to the position opening, or you can answer the question.

You will have to decide if you want to work for an employer who asks illegal questions. You can seek the advice of a personnel professional if you feel the need to report the incident.

Interview Thank-You Letters

Thank-you letters are an important part of the job search process; they can sometimes make or break a job offer. They should be sent immediately following an interview. Your thank-you letter can be typed on quality bond paper or hand written on a simple thank-you card. It must be legible and easy to read. Keep your thank-you letter brief and to the point.

Sample Thank-You Letter Outline

Date
Your name
Address

Employer's name
Title
Address

Dear _____,

Thank you for the opportunity to interview for the *position opening*. I enjoyed discussing how my education, skills, transferable skills, and experience would benefit *XYZ Company*. As a result of our meeting, I learned ….*give the employer one or two key points you learned. If you want to add something relevant you forgot during the interview, add the information here.*

I look forward to hearing from you regarding the position opening.

Sincerely,

Signature

Interview Rejection Letters

When not selected for a job, candidates will often receive a rejection letter from the employer. Your response to this letter can leave a potential employer with a favorable opinion of you even when another candidate has been selected. The individual who was offered the position may or may not accept it. If another position becomes available or the new employee doesn't work out, you may be offered the position at a later date.

Sample Rejection Letter Outline

Date
Your name
Address

Employer's name
Title
Address

Dear _____, (Target the individual who does the hiring.)

Paragraph I
My name is _____, and I interviewed for the position of _____, on ___ *(date)*. Although I understand another candidate has been selected, I wanted to let you know that I enjoyed meeting you and interviewing for the position. *XYZ* is an employer I would be proud to be associated with. *(explain why.)*

Paragraph II
Thank you again for your time and attention. If an opening becomes available in the future, I would appreciate another opportunity to interview.

Thank you for your consideration.

Sincerely,

Signature

Quick Tip

Submit a rejection follow-up letter only if you are still interested in the position. Prepare to contact the employer again within five to six months after your follow-up letter, in the event a new opportunity has become available.

ACKNOWLEDGMENTS

Special acknowledgments go to my mother, Lillie R. Sharon, daughter and son-in-law, Jennifer and Mark McCurry, for their support and feedback. Thank you to my son, Dennis Schmidt Jr., and grandchildren, Frances, Alex, Lily, and Zackery, to my brother, Lee Sharon, and nieces, Laura Greco and Veronica Sharon, and to Frank Santora, who patiently listened to me during the writing process, and Earl Ketry, my mentor, who encouraged me to complete the book.

A bravo goes to Editorial Assistant Jane Hauser and Editor Jane Killewald for their work and dedication to this project. Thank you to Thomas Millano, my web designer and Nicole Daly for the chapter graphic designs. A heartfelt thank-you to Sister Denise Roche, PhD, president of D'Youville College; to Robert Murphy and Jeffery Platt, for their encouragement; to Dr. Timothy Gallineau, who believed in the concept of the book; and to Tim Wiles, who helped create the book's title.

Appreciation is also extended to Zoltan Bereczty, L'Aszio Imre Hajdo, Christine Demcie, Helga Tyson, Jackie Krupczyk, Marcia Nowak, Mary Tisby, Nancy Shatzel, and Roberta Sampson.

A special thank-you goes to my Back on Track role models, Alisa Land, Cordell Porter, Dennis Kane, Julie Marinaccio, Kate Monroe, Kinga Mierzejewski, Larry Gatti, Margaret Clark, Milagrois Rodriguez, and Ted VanDueson.

Finally, my heart goes out to all of my former students and alumni who inspired me to write this book.

ABOUT THE AUTHOR

Frances Schmidt is a multifaceted student affairs administrator and author with career counseling, teaching, community service, and leadership experience. A proactive professional, Ms. Schmidt is dedicated to helping individuals accomplish their highest level of achievement and personal growth. Following twenty years of career counseling, including work as director of career services at D'Youville College in Buffalo, New York, she is currently the owner of F.R.S. Career & Retirement Counseling, providing individuals with assistance and direction in a variety of personal transitions.

Prior to her work on the college campus, Ms. Schmidt served as project associate/life education advisor for the University of Michigan at the Ford Stamping Plant in Buffalo. There she administered the Life Education Planning Program for more than two thousand UAW/Ford hourly workers, assisting employees with personal development planning and educational choices, as well as collaborating with local schools, colleges, agencies, and community groups to provide advice and support to company program members.

Again working on a college campus, but this time with adults, Ms. Schmidt served as adult admissions counselor at Hilbert College in Hamburg, New York, where she coordinated the adult recruitment program, including community career workshops and seminars.

Ms. Schmidt also worked as career counselor with Everywoman Opportunity Center in Buffalo, New York, an organization dedicated to providing career and employment assistance to women returning to the workplace. Here she implemented, evaluated, and coordinated an outreach career readiness program.

In 2000, Ms. Schmidt cofounded *Back on Track*, a career peer mentoring program of the Saint Vincent de Paul Society in Buffalo. This program provides opportunities for participants to gain confidence and to set personal and career goals in a supportive and nurturing environment. She continues to serve as volunteer coordinator.

As a career development educator, Ms. Schmidt has presented numerous career development workshops throughout the Western New York area. She is also the author of *Getting Hired in Any Job Market*.

Her education includes a master of science in student personnel administration from Buffalo State College, Buffalo. She earned both her bachelor of science in community and social services, concentration in counseling, and her associate of arts in human development from New York Empire State College, Buffalo.